Pg 27 - wordsearch
Pg 44-45 - working sheets (fun)
Pg 48-49 - working fun sheets
Pg 50-51 - work

THE AMAZING LIVERPOOL QUIZ

MASTERMIND CHALLENGE

JAMES CORMACK

AMAZING soccer BOOKS

CONTENTS

AMAZING LFC MEMBERS CLUB

Amazing LFC Members get free extracts of new books, free updates on new books.

Members are always the first to hear about my new books and publications.

At the back of the book there are details on how to sign up.

INTRODUCTION

Hello and Welcome to the **Amazing Liverpool Quiz**!

Here are 612 specially selected questions to test your memory, tease your brain, and heighten your appreciation of this confident and dominant club.

Liverpool have won pretty much everything that there is to win, at times in the most breathtaking of styles.

In football, as with life, we often wonder.

"What *might* have happened?"

What if pivotal events had turned out differently?

What if Bill Shankly had joined Everton instead of Liverpool in 1959?

What if Alex Ferguson had joined Liverpool instead of Man U in 1986?

The briefest of moments contain the power to change everything.

Of course we can't go back in time but, included at the back of this book, you will find a selection of alternative versions of history for Liverpool FC.

You should read the version that best matches your performance.

If you get most of the questions wrong, then you should take a glimpse of a miserable Liverpool reality.

If, on the other hand, you get most of the questions right, why not catch sight of an even more stellar version of Liverpool reality!

Beautiful success or wretched failure? What calibre of Reds history will *your* answers achieve?

One thing's for sure, this book has been designed for you to build a strong knowledge base of the most important people and events in the history of Liverpool.

The more you read this book, the more you will impress with your devotion and insight into what makes Liverpool, England's most feared and respected club.

You'll Never Walk Alone

WHY A QUIZ?

"As soon as I settle down into a quiz, I feel naturally relaxed. It's like I can just shut a door on the outside world and be in my own zone, testing my memory, and teasing my brain."

"I love the feeling of getting the answer right and now I time myself so it's even more challenging."

"I used to suffer from stress. A friend recommended I try quizzes so I did. Soon I find myself being able to retain information better, and focus on details more. I am glad I found quizzes. I do one every day now. Rain or shine."

As you grow older in life, it pays to keep your brain sharp, and stave off dementia and diseases such as Alzheimer's. Most elderly people report a failing memory. Memory loss can be as simple as forgetting where you put your keys to as serious as not knowing what day or even year it is.

Doing a quiz is a medically proven activity that helps you develop a strong memory. This is achieved by the ability of a quiz to reinforce existing connections between your brain cells.

With a healthy brain with healthy connections, you are in the best cognitive position to be in for your old age.

For young students - as the brain grows - it is even more beneficial to encourage the building of strong and improved neural networks as quizzes do.

Quizzes ensure the right attitude of fun towards learning. Quizzes are highly valued in top educational institutions as one of the best ways to engage students and enable learning in a fun way.

Quizzes can also help build confidence in your own ability to learn, and build motivation by immersing the learner in their chosen subject.

Those who do quizzes like this one from a very young age can expect to experience better performance in education, and an increased IQ.

In challenging times, a quiz is a way to keep your spirits and those of your family and friends high.

Doing a quiz, the participant has to think, dig deep, and, ultimately, be active.

So old Kopite or young Red, let the Liverpool learning fun begin!

QUESTION NUMBERS AND SECTIONS

Here are the number breakdowns for the sections of the quiz. Each section is comprised of one, two or three parts:

Section 1

Deep History (The Essence of Liverpool)

1A) **1-72** – **Foundations and Achievements**

1B) **73-159** -**Walking with Giants - Bill Shankly**

1C) **160-232 - Walking with Giants - Bob Paisley**

Section 2

Triumphs and Disasters (Eighties to Noughties)

2A) **233-398** - **The Red Machine**

2B) **399-470** - **Absolute Entertainment**

Section 3

Ultra-Modern Liverpool (Klopp & Co.)

3A) **470-612 - New Heights of Glory**

RANDOM NUMBER INSTRUCTIONS

1. Go to www.random.org

2. Type in the range of numbers that you want your selection to come from and generate as many questions as you like eg. 10, 30, 50, 100, 300

THE BEST WAYS TO PLAY AND LEARN

1. **Start to finish**

As an individual, the most natural and straightforward way to do the quiz is to simply work your way through it from start to finish.

2. **Tests and exams**

However in order for you to really drill down into the knowledge, selections of questions in the form of tests and exams can be great ways to learn even more effectively.

To follow this method, the first thing to do is to decide upon the length of your individual test or exam.

A test is just a miniature version of a full exam.

An exam is a thorough examination of the strength and depth of your knowledge.

Here are four examples of test and exam lengths:

Liverpool General Test

A 15 minute test comprising of 30 questions drawn completely at random from all 612 questions.

Liverpool Specialist Test

For example, a 15 minute test (specialised on a single chapter eg. The Red Machine)

Comprises of 30 questions drawn completely at random from questions numbered 233 to 398.

Liverpool Specialist Exam

For example, a 1 hour exam (specialised on a single section eg. Deep History)

Comprises of 100 questions drawn completely at random from questions numbered 1-232.

Liverpool General Exam

Comprises of 300 questions drawn completely at random from all 612 questions.

The Best of All Worlds

Possibly, the best way to learn all about LFC is to combine all of the above - go through each and every question one-by-one, and then revisit: challenge your memory of the answers by undertaking tests and exams, such as those indicated above.

As well as completing the above on your own, you can also organise individual and team competitions.

SUGGESTIONS FOR A TEAM OR INDIVIDUAL QUIZ

Have a Quiz Master

It is best for one person to take the responsibility of being the quiz master. This will ensure a neutral referee in case of dispute, and a focal point for the selection and asking of questions.

Have a Set of Rules

Here is an example set of rules for a team game that consists of two rounds.

General Rules

1. The decision of the quiz-master will be final and will not be subjected to any change.

2. The participants shall not be allowed to use mobile or other electronic instruments.

3. Questions to be asked by the quiz-master, with multiple choice answers provided.

THE AMAZING LIVERPOOL QUIZ

Competing in a team encourages social interaction and co-operation.

Two teams of three is a good number to ensure that everyone plays a role.

Two rounds provides variety.

Five minute first round

1. During the first round each team has to answer correctly as many questions as possible from their chosen section of the quiz (minimum range of 100) within five minutes.

2. If the five minutes expire just as the team is about to answer, they should be allowed to finish.

3. And similarly, if the question is in the process of being asked when the time runs out, it should be completed and answered.

Scoring for first round

1. 10 points for a correct answer

2. -5 points for a wrong answer (to discourage guessing)

30 Question second round

1. During the second round each team has to answer correctly 30 questions, and has a maximum of 30 seconds to answer, after being given all four possible answers.

Scoring for second round

1. A correct answer gets 10 points. If no correct answer is given, the opposing team gets the chance to answer correctly for 5 points.

The *Amazing Liverpool Quiz Team* is the team with the highest score after two rounds.

THE LIVERPOOL MASTERMIND QUIZ

Competing as an individual means that there is nowhere to hide if you lose, and you get all the credit if you win.

This quiz consists of two rounds that last as long as the participant continues to provide the correct answers.

Specialist Round One

The first round consists of questions from a chosen section of the Quiz (no more than 200 questions).

General Round Two

The second round consists of questions chosen at random from the entirety of the Quiz.

Lifeline

One lifeline per round can be used whereby two wrong answers are eliminated, and the participant can choose the correct answer from two alternatives.

Scoring

One point for each correct answer.

The *Liverpool Mastermind* is the winning individual who gets the most correct answers after the two rounds.

1. DEEP HISTORY

1A) FOUNDATIONS AND ACHIEVEMENTS

History

1. In which year was Liverpool FC founded?

A) 1878

B) 1888

C) 1892

D) 1899

2. Who founded Liverpool FC?

A) John Houlding

B) Joe Holmes

C) Peter Robinson

D) Tom Watson

3. In which league did Liverpool compete during their first season, 1892-93?

A) First Division

B) Second Division

C) Third Division

D) The Lancashire League

4. What was the name of the first stadium Liverpool played in?

A) Anfield

B) Blundell Park

C) Goodison Park

D) Prenton Park

5. Which year was Liverpool's first in the Football League?

A) 1890

B) 1893

C) 1896

D) 1899

6. How many English players were in the Liverpool team for the club's first ever match, a friendly against Rotherham?

A) 0

B) 3

C) 7

D) 11

7. How many Scottish players were in the Liverpool team for the club's first ever match?

A) 0

B) 3

C) 7

D) 11

8. How many fans turned up for Liverpool's first league match?

A) 200

B) 800

C) 8,000

D) 20,000

9. Which club played at Anfield before Liverpool?

A) Accrington Stanley

B) Bootle FC

C) Everton

D) Liverpool Stanley

10. What were Liverpool FC's first colours?

A) Blue shirts, white shorts

B) Blue and white chequered shirts and white shorts

C) Red shirts, white shorts

D) Red and white striped shirts and white shorts

11. When did Liverpool change to playing in all-red?

A) 1884

B) 1904

C) 1934

D) 1964

12. Which Liverpool legend retired in 1961 after signing with the club as a teenager in 1938?

A) Tommy Lawton

B) Billy Liddell

C) Stanley Matthews

D) Jimmy Melia

13. Which musical does the song *"You'll Never Walk Alone"* come from?

A) Carousel

B) Show Boat

C) The King & I

D) The Sound of Music

14. What is Liverpool FC's motto?

A) "Fortune Favours the Brave"

B) "God has Bestowed these Blessings on Us"

C) "Walking In The Air"

D) "You'll Never Walk Alone"

15. What is the main nickname of Liverpool FC?

A) The Reds

B) The Red Birds

C) The Red Imps

D) The Red Stars

Records and Statistics

16. Which Liverpool legend was the club's top scorer for seven out of eight seasons between 1927 and 1935?

A) Gordon Hodgson

B) Fred Howe

C) Billy Liddell

D) Jimmy Smith

17. For how many seasons was Billy Liddell the club's top scorer?

A) 1

B) 3

C) 5

D) 7

18. For how many seasons was Ian Rush the club's top scorer?

A) 2

B) 4

C) 6

D) 8

19. For how many seasons was Roger Hunt the club's top scorer?

A) 3

B) 6

C) 9

D) 12

20. For how many consecutive seasons was Michael Owen Liverpool's top scorer?

A) 1

B) 3

C) 5

D) 7

21. Which of the following players has never scored more than 40 goals in a season for Liverpool?

A) Roger Hunt

B) Michael Owen

C) Mo Salah

D) Ian Rush

22. After winning the Premier League title in 2020, what is the total number of Leagues, FA Cups, and League Cups Liverpool have won?

A) 30

B) 34

C) 38

D) 42

23. As of 2020, what is the total number of European Cups, Champions Leagues, Europa Leagues, UEFA Cup Winners' Cups, UEFA Super Cups, Intercontinental Cups, and FIFA Club World Cups that Liverpool have won?

A) 10

B) 12

C) 14

D) 16

24. Who was Liverpool's first shirt sponsor?

A) Hitachi

B) Panasonic

C) Sony

D) Toshiba

25. Which of the following companies has not been the shirt sponsor of Liverpool?

A) Candy

B) Carlsberg

C) Crown Paints

D) Philips

26. Which Liverpool player scored a hat-trick of penalties in an FA Cup tie against Coventry in 1986?

A) Kenny Dalglish

B) Jan Molby

C) Ian Rush

D) Ronnie Whelan

27. What is Liverpool's record victory?

A) 10-1

B) 11-0

C) 12-1

D) 13-0

28. Who were Liverpool's opponents when the club recorded its record victory?

A) Macclesfield

B) Norrkoping

C) Rotherham

D) Stromsgodset

29. Who is the only Liverpool player to have been awarded the Ballon D'Or?

A) Steven Gerrard

B) Roger Hunt

C) Michael Owen

D) Luis Suarez

30. Who has scored the most goals for Liverpool?

A) Robbie Fowler

B) Roger Hunt

C) Michael Owen

D) Ian Rush

31. Which Liverpool player has made the most consecutive appearances for the club?

A) David James

B) Alan Kennedy

C) Mark Lawrenson

D) Phil Neal

32. Which of the following Liverpool players has scored the most hat-tricks for the club?

A) Robbie Fowler

B) Gordon Hodgson

C) Ian Rush

D) Luis Suarez

33. What was the average age of the Liverpool side that played Aston Villa away in the League Cup in 2019?

A) 18.5

B) 19.5

C) 21.5

D) 23.5

34. What was the final score of that match?

A) Liverpool won 0-2

B) Liverpool won 0-4

C) Liverpool lost 0-3

D) Liverpool lost 5-0

35. Which non-English player has the most appearances for Liverpool?

A) Kenny Dalglish

B) Alan Hansen

C) Mark Lawrenson

D) Ian Rush

36. Which non-British player has the most appearances for Liverpool?

A) Bruce Grobbelaar

B) Sami Hypia

C) John-Arne Riise

D) Arthur Riley

37. In which of the following seasons did Liverpool win their first top flight league title?

A) 1898-1899

B) 1899-1900

C) 1900-1901

D) 1901-1902

38. In which of the following decades did Liverpool win back-to-back league titles?

A) 1900s

B) 1910s

C) 1920s

D) 1930s

39. In which of the following decades did Liverpool win a league title?

A) 1930s

B) 1940s

C) 2000s

D) 2010s

40. In which decade did Liverpool win their first FA Cup?

A) 1940s

B) 1950s

C) 1960s

D) 1970s

41. In which of the following decades did Liverpool win the most league titles?

A) 1950s

B) 1960s

C) 1970s

D) 1980s

42. In which decade did Liverpool win their first League Cup?

A) 1950s

B) 1960s

C) 1970s

D) 1980s

43. In which decade did Liverpool win their first European trophy?

A) 1950s

B) 1960s

C) 1970s

D) 1980s

44. Which of the following players has scored the most goals for Liverpool in a season?

A) Gordon Hodgson

B) Michael Owen

C) Ian Rush

D) Mo Salah

45. How many players have Liverpool sold for more than they spent on Virgil Van Dijk?

A) 0

B) 1

C) 2

D) 3

Anfield

46. What are the names of the four stands at Liverpool's home ground?

A) The Spion Kop, the East Stand, the sir Kenny Dalglish Stand, the Anfield Road End

B) The Spion Kop, the Main Stand, the Sir Kenny Dalglish Stand, the Anfield Road End

C) The Spion Kop, the North Stand, the Sir Kenny Dalglish Stand, the Anfield Road End

D) The Spion Kop, the South Stand, the Sir Kenny Dalglish Stand, the Anfield Road End

47. What is the highest attendance recorded at Anfield?

A) 48,865

B) 55,789

C) 61,905

D) 69,755

48. Who were Liverpool's opponents for that match?

A) AC Milan

B) Everton

C) Real Madrid

D) Wolves

49. What was the final score of that match?

A) 0-0

B) 1-1

C) 2-1

D) 1-2 (to their opponents)

50. In which year were floodlights installed at Anfield?

A) 1917

B) 1937

C) 1957

D) 1977

51. What is the current capacity of Liverpool's home ground?

A) 49,964

B) 54,074

C) 59,795

D) 63,765

52. What are the words that read across the Shankly Gate?

A) “Strength In Unity”

B) “To Dare Is To Do”

C) “When You Walk Through A Storm”

D) “You’ll Never Walk Alone”

Skippers

53. Who was Liverpool captain from 1961-70?

A) Billy Liddell

B) Ronnie Moran

C) Ian St John

D) Ron Yeats

54. Who was Liverpool captain from 1970-73?

A) Ray Kennedy

B) Tommy Smith

C) John Toshack

D) Johnny Wheeler

55. Who was Liverpool captain from 1973-78?

A) Ian Callaghan

B) Ray Clemence

C) Emlyn Hughes

D) John Toshack

56. Who was Liverpool captain from 1978-81?

A) Alan Kennedy

B) Ray Kennedy

C) Phil Thompson

D) Ray Clemence

57. Who was Liverpool captain from 1982-84?

A) Alan Hansen

B) Mark Lawrenson

C) Phil Neal

D) Graeme Souness

58. Who was Liverpool captain from 1985-88?

A) Kenny Dalglish

B) Gary Gillespie

C) Alan Hansen

D) Steve Nicol

59. Who was Liverpool captain from 1993-96?

A) John Barnes

B) Steve Nicol

C) Ian Rush

D) Mark Wright

60. Who was Liverpool captain from 1996-97?

A) Phil Babb

B) John Barnes

C) Robbie Fowler

D) Paul Ince

61. Who was Liverpool captain from 1999-2002?

A) Jamie Carragher

B) Robbie Fowler

C) Sami Hypia

D) Jamie Redknapp

62. Who was Liverpool captain from 2003-15?

A) John Aarne Riise

B) Jamie Carragher

C) Steven Gerrard

D) Dietmar Hamann

In Quotes

63. Which Liverpool player said the following?

"Sometimes you open your mouth and it punches you straight between the eyes."

A) John Aldridge

B) Peter Beardsley

C) Ian Rush

D) Nigel Spackman

64. Which Liverpool manager made the following statement when asked about his likely team selection?

"I'm not giving secrets like that to Milan. If I had my way I wouldn't even tell them the time of the kick-off."

A) Kenny Dalglish

B) Joe Fagan

C) Bob Paisley

D) Bill Shankly

65. Who had this to say about playing at Anfield?

"When they start singing *"You'll Never Walk Alone"* my eyes start to water. There have been times when I've actually been crying while I've been playing."

A) Peter Beardsley

B) Kenny Dalglish

C) Kevin Keegan

D) Ian Rush

66. Which Liverpool manager said the following?

"I use a quote with the players, "per aspera ad astra", which is Latin for "through adversity to the stars."

A) Rafa Benitez

B) Roy Hodgson

C) Gerard Houllier

D) Brendan Rodgers

67. Which Liverpool manager said the following?

“One of the things I keep reminding players is that when you’re lost in a fog, you must stick together.”

A) Roy Hodgson

B) Bob Paisley

C) Bill Shankly

D) Graeme Souness

68. Which Liverpool manager made the following statement?

“You can live without water for many days, but you can’t live for a second without hope.”

A) Jurgen Klopp

B) Brendan Rodgers

C) Bill Shankly

D) Graeme Souness

69. Who said this?

"I was the best manager in Britain because I was never devious or cheated anyone. I'd break my wife's legs if I played against her, but I'd never cheat her."

A) Kenny Dalglish

B) Bob Paisley

C) Bill Shankly

D) Graeme Souness

70. Which Liverpool manager said the following?

"Newspapers remind me of Jaws. They'll consume anything you've got and be back for more the next day."

A) Kenny Dalglish

B) Joe Fagan

C) Bob Paisley

D) Bill Shankly

71. Who said the following?

"A football team is like a piano. You need eight men to carry it and three to play the damn thing."

A) Kenny Dalglish

B) Joe Fagan

C) Bob Paisley

D) Bill Shankly

72. Which Liverpool legend made the following statement?

“This club has been my life: I’d go out and sweep the street and be proud to do it for Liverpool FC if they asked me to.”

A) Ian Callaghan

B) Jamie Carragher

C) Steven Gerrard

D) Bob Paisley

1B) WALKING WITH GIANTS - BILL SHANKLY

Leader and Inspiration

73. What was Bill Shankly's nationality?

A) English

B) Irish

C) Northern Irish

D) Scottish

74. How many appearances did he make for his country?

A) 5

B) 25

C) 35

D) 55

75. What was Shankly's playing position?

A) Central-defence

B) Centre-forward

C) Left-half

D) Right-half

76. Which team did Shankly spend the majority of his playing career with?

A) Carlisle United

B) Huddersfield Town

C) Preston North End

D) Raith Rovers

77. What did Shankly win as a player?

A) League title, FA Cup

B) League title

C) FA Cup

D) League Cup

78. In which year did Bill Shankly join Liverpool as manager?

A) 1957

B) 1959

C) 1961

D) 1963

79. Which club was he the manager of before he joined Liverpool?

A) Carlisle United

B) Grimsby Town

C) Huddersfield Town

D) Preston North End

80. What was the first trophy Shankly won as Liverpool manager?

A) First Division Champions

B) Second Division title

C) Third Division title

D) League Cup

81. In which year did Shankly resign as Liverpool manager?

A) 1974

B) 1976

C) 1978

D) 1980

82. What trophies did Bill Shankly win with Liverpool?

A) 1 First Division title, 1 Second Division title, 1 Third Division title, 2 FA Cups, 3 FA Charity Shields, 1 UEFA Cup, 1 European Cup

B) 2 First Division titles, 2 FA Cups, 3 FA Charity Shields, 2 UEFA Cups

C) 3 First Division titles, 1 Second Division title, 2 FA Cups, 3 FA Charity Shields, 1 UEFA Cup

D) 4 First Division titles, 1 Second Division title, 2 FA Cups, 3 FA Charity Shields

83. After which game did Bill Shankly say the following?

"Sickness would not have kept me away from this one. If I'd been dead, I would have had them bring the casket to the ground, prop it up in the stands and cut a hole in the lid."

A) 1971 FA Cup Semi-final

B) 1973 UEFA Cup Final

C) 1977 European Cup Final

D) 1978 European Cup Final

84. What did Bill Shankly say when asked "is it true you would tackle your own grandmother if necessary?"

A) "Don't be stupid. She would have more sense than to come anywhere near me."

B) "How dare you? I would never be so stupid. I wouldn't have to tackle her, I would make sure that she'd hardly get a touch of the ball."

C) "If necessary, but I would take it a little easy on her. She is 98 after all!"

D) "When it comes to football, I'll tackle anyone, even the Queen!"

85. Who was Bill Shankly's favourite actor?

A) James Cagney

B) Sean Connery

C) Cary Grant

D) James Stewart

86. What are the words inscribed under the statue of Bill Shankly outside Anfield?

A) "He made the people happy"

B) "Simply the Best"

C) "The Leader of Liverpool"

D) "You'll Never Walk Alone"

87. Which defender, signed from Dundee United by Bill Shankly, became the rock of the Liverpool defence?

A) Emlyn Hughes

B) Larry Lloyd

C) Tommy Smith

D) Ron Yeats

88. Which player was Bill Shankly's most expensive signing for Liverpool?

A) Kevin Keegan

B) Alan Kennedy

C) Ray Kennedy

D) John Toshack

89. Who became the most expensive teenager ever signed when they joined Liverpool from Wolves in September 1968 for £110,000?

A) Alun Evans

B) Tony Hateley

C) Sammy Reid

D) Billy Wright

90. Which one of Bill Shankly's players said the following?

"We do things together. I'd walk into the toughest dockside pub in the world with this lot because you know that if things got tough, nobody would bottle it and scoot off."

A) Ray Clemence

B) Emlyn Hughes

C) Kevin Keegan

D) Ron Yeats

91. To which player did Bill Shankly say the following?

"Look laddie, if you're in the penalty area and not quite sure what to do with the ball, just stick it in the net and we'll discuss your options afterwards."

A) Tony Hateley

B) Kevin Keegan

C) Ian St John

D) John Toshack

92. Which Liverpool player, according to Bill Shankly, “would start a riot in a graveyard”?

A) Emlyn Hughes

B) Kevin Keegan

C) Tommy Smith

D) Ron Yeats

93. Which Liverpool player was known as the “Flying Pig”?

A) Ray Clemence

B) Tommy Lawrence

C) Tommy Lawton

D) Tommy Smith

Roger Hunt

94. In which year was Hunt born?

A) 1918

B) 1928

C) 1938

D) 1948

95. Who was the manager who signed Hunt for Liverpool?

A) Bob Paisley

B) Bill Shankly

C) Phil Taylor

D) Don Welsh

96. In which tier of English football were the Anfield club in at the time?

A) First

B) Second

C) Third

D) Fourth

97. How many league games did Hunt play for Liverpool?

A) 202

B) 303

C) 404

D) 505

98. How many league goals did he score for Liverpool?

A) 134

B) 245

C) 356

D) 467

99. What did Hunt win for Liverpool?

A) 2 First Division titles, 1 Second Division title, 1 Third Division title 1 FA Cup, 3 FA Charity Shields

B) 2 First Division titles, 1 Second Division title, 1 FA Cup, 3 FA Charity Shields

C) 1 First Division title, 1 Second Division title, 1 Third Division title, 1 Fourth Division title 2 FA Cups, 3 FA Charity Shields

D) 1 First Division title, 1 Second Division title, 2 FA Cups, 1 League Cup, 1 UEFA Cup, 3 FA Charity Shields

100. How many games did Roger Hunt play for England?

A) 24

B) 34

C) 44

D) 54

101. How many goals did he score for England?

A) 18

B) 24

C) 30

D) 42

102. What did he win with England?

A) Nothing

B) World Cup

C) European Championship

D) World Cup and European Championship

103. For how many years did Roger Hunt play for Liverpool?

A) 7 years

B) 11 years

C) 15 years

D) 17 years

104. Which club did Hunt join after leaving Liverpool?

A) Blackburn

B) Blackpool

C) Bolton Wanderers

D) Everton

105. What profession did Hunt enter after football?

A) Construction

B) Electrician

C) Haulage

D) Painting and decorating

106. Who said this?

"Roger Hunt is a player's player. He is possibly appreciated more by those who play with him and against him than by those who watch him."

A) Bobby Charlton

B) Emlyn Hughes

C) Bobby Moore

D) Ian St John

107. What playing attributes did Hunt have?

A) Attacking midfielder with ability to make runs from deep and find space to score goals

B) Quick, strong, skilful, with a powerful shot

C) Strong tackling defensive midfielder with ability to shoot powerfully from distance

D) Tricky winger with the ability to both set up goals and score

1963-64 First Division

108. Liverpool were crowned Champions of England in 1964. The triumph meant that the Reds had won the league title how many times?

A) 2

B) 3

C) 5

D) 6

109. Which year had seen Liverpool's most recent First Division title before they won it in 1964?

A) 1927

B) 1937

C) 1947

D) 1951

110. Which team finished second in the First Division in 1963-64?

A) Leeds United

B) Man U

C) Sheffield Wednesday

D) West Ham

111. Who was Liverpool's leading goalscorer during 1963-64?

A) Roger Hunt

B) Gordon Hodgson

C) Kevin Keegan

D) John Toshack

112. Which three players played every league game for Liverpool in 1963-64?

A) Ian Callaghan, Gordon Milne, Peter Thompson

B) Roger Hunt, Tommy Lawrence, Ian St John

C) Willie Stevenson, Ron Yeats, Ronnie Moran

D) John Toshack, John Charles, Tommy Lawton

113. What was the most recent trophy Liverpool had won before they lifted the First Division title in 1964?

A) FA Cup

B) League Cup

C) Second Division Title

D) Third Division Title

114. Who scored four second-half goals against Stoke City on Boxing Day 1963?

A) Gordon Hodgson

B) Roger Hunt

C) Kevin Keegan

D) John Toshack

1965 FA Cup

115. Who did Liverpool beat en-route to the 1965 FA Cup final?

A) Birmingham City, Tranmere Rovers, Everton, Crystal Palace, Man U

B) Southport, Birmingham City, Shrewsbury Town, Everton, Chelsea

C) Southport, Everton, Shrewsbury Town, Crystal Palace, Man U

D) West Brom, Stockport, Bolton Wanderers, Leicester City, Chelsea

116. Who did Liverpool's final opponents, Leeds, beat in their semi-final?

A) Chelsea

B) Everton

C) Man City

D) Man United

117. What was the half-time score in the 1965 FA Cup final?

A) 0-0

B) 1-0

C) 1-1

D) 2-1

118. What was the full-time score in the 1965 FA Cup final?

A) 2-1

B) 3-1

C) 3-2

D) 4-3

119. Who were the Liverpool goalscorers in the 1965 FA Cup final?

A) Hunt, Smith, and Thompson

B) Hunt and Smith

C) Hunt and St John

D) Smith, St John, and Thompson

120. Who was the Leeds manager and goalscorer?

A) Brian Clough and Joe Jordan

B) Brian Clough and Peter Lorimer

C) Don Revie and Allan Clarke

D) Don Revie and Billy Bremner

Emlyn Hughes

121. Where was Emlyn Hughes born?

A) Bangor

B) Barrow-in-Furness

C) Blackpool

D) Bristol

122. What is Hughes's date of birth?

A) 25th May 1944

B) 26th June 1945

C) 27th July 1946

D) 28th August 1947

123. What is his full name?

A) Emlyn Archibald Hughes

B) Emlyn Bartholemew Hughes

C) Emlyn Reginald Montgomery Hughes

D) Emlyn Walter Hughes

124. Who did Hughes play for before Liverpool?

A) Bangor

B) Blackpool

C) Brighton

D) Bristol City

125. In which year did Hughes sign for Liverpool?

A) 1959

B) 1963

C) 1967

D) 1971

126. In which tier of English football were the Anfield club in at the time?

A) First

B) Second

C) Third

D) Fourth

127. What was Hughes's nickname at Liverpool?

A) Crazy Horse

B) The Rock

C) The Wall

D) Wild Animal

128. What did Hughes win with Liverpool?

A) 4 League titles, 1 FA Cup, 3 FA Charity Shields, 2 European Cups, 2 UEFA Cups, 1 UEFA Super Cup

B) 4 League titles, 1 Second Division title, 1 FA Cup, 3 FA Charity Shields, 2 European Cups, 1 UEFA Cup, 1 UEFA Super Cup

C) 3 League titles, 1 Second Division title, 1 Third Division title 2 FA Cups, 3 FA Charity Shields, 1 European Cup, 2 UEFA Cups

D) 2 League titles, 1 Second Division title, 1 Third Division title, 1 Fourth Division title, 2 FA Cup, 3 FA Charity Shields, 3 European Cups, 1 UEFA Cups, 1 UEFA Super Cup

129. Which club did Hughes join after Liverpool?

A) Blackpool

B) Bristol City

C) Rotherham

D) Wolverhampton Wanderers

130. How many England caps did he win?

A) 62

B) 72

C) 82

D) 92

131. Which club did Emlyn Hughes manage?

A) Blackpool

B) Bristol City

C) Rotherham United

D) Wolverhampton

132. Which BBC television program was Hughes a regular on in the 1980s?

A) Match of the Day

B) Question Time

C) A Question of Sport

D) Sportsnight

133. What were the attributes of Hughes's game?

A) Coolness, calmness, composure. An assassin in front of goal. One of the most dangerous strikers in the world, on his day

B) Energy, intensity, will-to-win, surging forward, tackling, anticipation

C) A flamboyant, eccentric genius. Able to create goalscoring chances out of nothing. Scorer of great goals, often coming at the end of long, mazy dribbles

D) A hard-running player able to man-mark players out of the game, and whip in crosses that were unerringly accurate

D) Physically aggressive, consistent. Hard-working, hard-tackling. A complete midfielder who could also pass the ball well, dictate the tempo of the game, and score goals from range

Kevin Keegan

134. Where was Kevin Keegan born?

A) Dagenham

B) Doncaster

C) Dunstable

D) Durham

135. Where are Keegan's ancestors from?

A) France

B) Ireland

C) Italy

D) Wales

136. In which year was he born?

A) 1947

B) 1951

C) 1955

D) 1959

137. Who did Keegan support as a boy?

A) Doncaster Rovers

B) Newcastle

C) Scunthorpe

D) Southampton

138. From which club did Liverpool sign Kevin Keegan?

A) Newcastle

B) Scunthorpe

C) Southampton

D) Sunderland

139. In which year was Keegan signed?

A) 1961

B) 1966

C) 1971

D) 1976

140. What was the transfer fee that Liverpool paid to sign Keegan?

A) £33,000

B) £77,000

C) £125,000

D) £175,000

141. How many (total) games did Keegan play for Liverpool?

A) 224

B) 274

C) 324

D) 374

142. How many (total) goals did Keegan score for Liverpool in total?

A) 52

B) 92

C) 122

D) 174

143. What did Liverpool win while Kevin Keegan was at the club?

A) 3 League titles, 1 FA Cup, 2 Charity Shields, 2 European Cups, 2 UEFA Cups

B) 3 League titles, 1 FA Cup, 2 Charity Shields, 1 European Cup, 2 UEFA Cups

C) 2 League titles, 1 Second Division title, 1 FA Cup, 2 Charity Shields, 2 European Cups, 2 UEFA Cups

D) 2 League titles, 1 FA Cup, 2 Charity Shields, 1 European Cup, 1 UEFA Cup

144. In which year did Keegan leave Liverpool?

A) 1977

B) 1979

C) 1981

D) 1984

145. Who signed Keegan from Liverpool?

A) Borussia Monchengladbach

B) Hamburg

C) Newcastle United

D) Southampton

146. What was the transfer fee that Liverpool received when they sold Keegan?

A) £500,000

B) £700,000

C) £900,000

D) £1,100,000

147. Which national team did Keegan play for?

A) England

B) Ireland

C) Scotland

D) Wales

148. How many caps did Keegan win for his country?

A) 51

B) 63

C) 75

D) 87

149. How many goals did he score for his country?

A) 21

B) 35

C) 42

D) 53

150. How many Ballon D'Ors did Keegan win?

A) 0

B) 1

C) 2

D) 3

151. What position did Keegan play in for Liverpool?

A) Centre-back

B) Centre-midfield

C) Left-back

D) Forward

152. What were his playing attributes?

A) Attacking full back with an eye for goal

B) Midfield playmaker with ability to play killer pass

C) Slow, calm, passing midfielder

D) Speed, stamina, work-rate, athleticism, strength, goal-scoring

1974 FA Cup

153. Who did Liverpool beat en-route to the 1974 FA Cup final?

A) Doncaster Rovers, Carlisle United, Ipswich Town, Bristol City, Leicester City

B) Doncaster Rovers, Scunthorpe United, Ipswich Town, Nottingham Forest, Leicester City

C) West Brom, Carlisle United, Bristol City, Nottingham Forest, Derby County

D) West Brom, Scarborough, Bournemouth, Nottingham Forest, Derby County

154. Who did Liverpool play in the 1974 FA Cup final?

A) Leeds

B) Newcastle United

C) Sunderland

D) Spurs

155. Who was the manager of Liverpool's opposition in the 1974 FA Cup final?

A) Colin Harvey

B) David Harvey

C) Frank Harvey

D) Joe Harvey

156. What was the half-time score in the 1974 FA Cup final?

A) 0-0

B) 1-0

C) 2-0

D) 3-0

157. What was the final score of the 1974 FA Cup final?

A) 3-0

B) 4-0

C) 5-0

D) 6-0

158. Who scored for Liverpool in the 1974 FA Cup final?

A) Kevin Keegan, Steve Heighway

B) Kevin Keegan, Steve Heighway, John Toshack

C) Steve Heighway, John Toshack

D) John Toshack

159. Which two players who lined up against Liverpool in the 1974 FA Cup final later became Liverpool players?

A) Pat Howard and Bobby Moncur

B) Alan Kennedy and Terry McDermott

C) Willie McFaul and Frank Clark

D) Jimmy Smith and Tommy Cassidy

1C) WALKING WITH GIANTS - BOB PAISLEY

The Winning Formula

160. Where was Bob Paisley born?

A) County Durham

B) Durban

C) Leeds

D) Manchester

161. What position did Bob Paisley play in for Liverpool?

A) Centre Half

B) Left Half

C) Right Half

D) Centre midfield

162. What is Paisley's date of birth?

A) 23rd January 1914

B) 23rd January 1919

C) 23rd January 1924

D) 23rd January 1929

163. In which year did Liverpool sign Paisley as a player?

A) 1934

B) 1939

C) 1945

D) 1947

164. In which year did Paisley make his debut for Liverpool?

A) 1945

B) 1946

C) 1947

D) 1948

165. What did Paisley win as a player for Liverpool?

A) First Division title

B) Second Division title

C) Third Division title

D) FA Cup

166. When did Bob Paisley join the back-room staff at Liverpool?

A) 1954

B) 1959

C) 1964

D) 1969

167. What was Paisley's official title when he joined the back-room?

A) Assistant Manager

B) First Team Coach

C) Physiotherapist

D) Tactician

168. When Bill Shankly retired what was Paisley's official title at Liverpool?

A) Assistant Manager

B) First Team Coach

C) Physiotherapist

D) Tactician

169. In which year did Paisley take over as manager of Liverpool FC?

A) 1973

B) 1974

C) 1975

D) 1976

170. In which year did Paisley retire as Liverpool manager?

A) 1979

B) 1981

C) 1983

D) 1985

171. What did he win as Liverpool manager?

A) 3 First Division titles, 4 League Cups, 2 FA Cups, 6 FA Charity Shields, 2 European Cups, 1 UEFA Cup, 1 European Cup Winners' Cups

B) 4 First Division titles, 3 League Cups, 6 FA Charity Shields, 4 European Cups, 1 European Super Cup

C) 5 First Division titles, 3 League Cups, 6 FA Charity Shields, 2 European Cups, 2 UEFA Cups, 1 European Super Cup

D) 6 First Division titles, 3 League Cups, 6 FA Charity Shields, 3 European Cups, 1 UEFA Cup, 1 European Super Cup

172. Which one of Paisley's players said this about his manager?

"We didn't know what he was talking about half the time but we knew what he wanted."

A) Emlyn Hughes

B) Kevin Keegan

C) Tommy Smith

D) Phil Thompson

173. Who was Paisley's most expensive signing for Liverpool?

A) Kenny Dalglish

B) Alan Hansen

C) Mark Lawrenson

D) Ian Rush

174. What was the transfer fee that Liverpool paid to bring Paisley's most expensive signing to the club?

A) £700,000

B) £800,000

C) £900,000

D) £1,000,000

175. In which year did the transfer take place?

A) 1975

B) 1977

C) 1979

D) 1981

176. Which player, signed by Bob Paisley from Partick Thistle, went on to make 620 appearances for the Reds?

A) Kenny Dalglish

B) Gary Gillespie

C) Alan Hansen

D) Steve Nicol

1976-77 European Cup

177. Liverpool's capture of the 1976-77 European Cup was the third time the competition had been won by a British football club. Which was the first British team to lift the trophy?

A) Arsenal

B) Celtic

C) Man U

D) Spurs

178. It was Liverpool's second European trophy. In which year did Liverpool win its first European trophy?

A) 1969

B) 1970

C) 1973

D) 1974

179. Which club did Liverpool beat in the 1977 European Cup final?

A) Bayern Munich

B) Borussia Monchengladbach

C) Hamburg

D) St Etienne

180. What was the half-time score in the 1977 European Cup final?

A) 0-0

B) 1-0 to Liverpool

C) 0-1 to their opponents

D) 1-1

181. What was the final score of the 1977 European Cup final?

A) 2-0

B) 3-0

C) 2-1

D) 3-1

182. Where was the 1977 European Cup final played?

A) Olympic Stadium, Athens

B) Olympiastadion, Munich

C) San Siro, Milan

D) Stadio Olimpico, Rome

183. Who were the Liverpool goalscorers in the 1977 European Cup final?

A) Case, Callaghan, Kennedy

B) Heighway, Kennedy

C) Keegan, Jones

D) McDermott, Smith, Neal

184. Who were Liverpool's joint top-scorers in the tournament with four goals each?

A) Heighway and McDermott

B) Heighway and Neal

C) Keegan and Kennedy

D) Keegan and Neal

Kenny Dalglish

185. When was Kenny Dalglish born?

A) 1st March 1950

B) 4th March 1951

C) 7th March 1952

D) 10th March 1953

186. What is his middle name?

A) Amadeus

B) Ambrose

C) Matthias

D) Mathieson

187. Which club did Dalglish support as a child?

A) Celtic

B) Man U

C) Liverpool

D) Rangers

188. Which was the first club that Dalglish played for?

A) Celtic

B) Dundee

C) Dundee United

D) Rangers

189. In which year did Liverpool sign Dalglish to play for the club?

A) 1976

B) 1977

C) 1978

D) 1979

190. Who was the player that Dalglish was signed by Liverpool to replace?

A) David Fairclough

B) Kevin Keegan

C) Ray Kennedy

D) John Toshack

191. What was the transfer fee that Liverpool paid to secure Dalglish's services as a player?

A) £330,000

B) £440,000

C) £550,000

D) £660,000

192. How many (total) appearances did Dalglish make as a player for Liverpool?

A) 335

B) 355

C) 475

D) 505

193. How many goals did Dalglish score for Liverpool in total?

A) 129

B) 169

C) 209

D) 249

194. In which year did Kenny Dalglish become player-manager of Liverpool?

A) 1983

B) 1985

C) 1987

D) 1989

195. What achievement did Dalglish accomplish in his first season as player-manager that was unprecedented for Liverpool?

A) League and FA Cup Double

B) League and European Cup Double

C) FA and European Cup Double

D) FA Cup and League Cup Double

196. What did Liverpool win with Dalglish (as player and as manager)?

A) 5 League titles, 4 FA Cups, 5 League Cups, 8 Charity Shields (2 shared), 2 European Cups, 2 UEFA Cups, 2 European Super Cups, 1 Football League Super Cup

B) 6 League titles, 3 FA Cups, 5 League Cups, 8 Charity Shields (2 shared), 3 European Cups, 1 UEFA Cup, 1 European Super Cup, 1 Football League Super Cup

C) 7 League titles, 3 FA Cups, 4 League Cups, 8 Charity Shields (2 shared), 4 European Cups, 1 European Super Cup, 1 Football League Super Cup

D) 8 League titles, 2 FA Cups, 5 League Cups, 8 Charity Shields (2 shared), 3 European Cups, 1 European Super Cup, 1 Football League Super Cup

197. What two pieces of advice did Bill Shankly give to Dalglish when he arrived in Liverpool?

A) "Don't over-eat and don't lose your accent"

B) "Pass and move"

C) "Play for the love of the game and play to win"

D) "Train hard and sleep well"

198. What were Dalglish's playing attributes?

A) All-round, versatile box-to-box midfielder, capable of playing anywhere in midfield

B) Intelligence, consistency, passing, shooting

C) Hard-working physical midfielder, strong tackler, good passer, leader, motivator, organiser

D) Tricky winger who used pace and power to bomb forward at every available opportunity. Master of the banana free-kick that would curl wickedly and find its way past the keeper into the net

1977-78 European Cup

199. Who did Liverpool beat en-route to the 1978 European Cup final?

A) Dinamo Bucharest, Benfica, Borussia Dortmund

B) Dinamo Kiev, Benfica, Bayern Munich

C) Dinamo Kiev, Borussia Dortmund, Benfica

D) Dynamo Dresden, Benfica, Borussia Monchengladbach

200. In which country was the 1978 European Cup final played?

A) England

B) Netherlands

C) Spain

D) West Germany

201. Who were Liverpool's opponents in the 1978 European Cup final?

A) Anderlecht

B) Cercle Brugge

C) Club Brugge

D) Standard Liege

202. What was the half-time score in the 1978 European Cup final?

A) 0-0

B) 0-1 (to their opponents)

C) 1-1

D) 2-1

203. What was the final score of the 1978 European Cup final?

A) 1-0

B) 2-1

C) 3-2

D) 4-2

204. Who scored the winning goal of the 1978 European Cup final?

A) Jimmy Case

B) Kenny Dalglish

C) David Fairclough

D) Ray Kennedy

205. Who was Liverpool's leading goalscorer in the 1977-78 European Cup competition?

A) Jimmy Case

B) Kenny Dalglish

C) David Fairclough

D) Ray Kennedy

Graeme Souness

206. What is Souness's full name?

A) Graeme Kenneth Souness

B) Graeme James Souness

C) Graeme Matthew John Souness

D) Graeme William Souness

207. In which city was Graeme Souness born?

A) Dundee

B) Dunfermline

C) Edinburgh

D) Glasgow

208. Which two clubs did Souness support as a child?

A) Celtic and Hearts

B) Hearts and Rangers

C) Hibs and St Mirren

D) Rangers and Celtic

209. At which club did Graeme Souness start his football playing career?

A) Celtic

B) Spurs

C) St Mirren

D) Rangers

210. Who did Liverpool sign Souness from as a player?

A) Celtic

B) Hibs

C) Middlesbrough

D) Rangers

211. In which year did Liverpool sign Souness to play for the club?

A) 1977

B) 1978

C) 1979

D) 1980

212. What was the transfer fee that Liverpool paid to sign Souness?

A) £152,000

B) £252,000

C) £352,000

D) £452,000

213. In which year was Souness made Liverpool captain?

A) 1980

B) 1981

C) 1982

D) 1983

214. Who did Souness take over the Liverpool captain's armband from?

A) Kenny Dalglish

B) Alan Kennedy

C) Phil Neal

D) Phil Thompson

215. How many (total) appearances did Souness make for Liverpool?

A) 359

B) 409

C) 429

D) 479

216. How many (total) goals did he score for Liverpool?

A) 55

B) 75

C) 105

D) 145

217. What did Souness win as a Liverpool player?

A) 4 League titles, 2 League Cups, 3 FA Charity Shields, 2 European Cups

B) 5 League titles, 3 League Cups, 3 FA Charity Shields, 3 European Cups

C) 6 League titles, 4 League Cups, 3 FA Charity Shields, 2 European Cups

D) 7 League titles, 2 FA Cups, 3 FA Charity Shields, 1 European Cup, 1 European Super Cup

218. Who did Souness leave Liverpool to play for?

A) Aston Villa

B) Benfica

C) Middlesbrough

D) Sampdoria

219. In which year did Souness return to Anfield as manager?

A) 1991

B) 1993

C) 1995

D) 1997

220. Who was Souness's immediate predecessor as Liverpool manager?

A) Kenny Dalglish

B) Roy Evans

C) Gerard Houllier

D) Ronnie Moran

221. In which year did Souness resign from the Liverpool manager post?

A) 1994

B) 1997

C) 2000

D) 2003

222. What did Souness win as manager of Liverpool?

A) Nothing

B) FA Cup

C) League Cup

D) League Title

223. What were Graeme Souness's playing attributes?

A) Aggressive, powerful, strong tackler, passing range, strong runner, attacking drive

B) Intelligent, tactically aware leader who plays just behind the forwards with a prolific goalscoring and assist-making rate

C) Tricky winger with pace to burn

D) Consistently excellent full-back who is known for cutting inside and scoring stupendous goals from very long distances

1980-81 European Cup

224. Who were the defending European Champions going into the 1980-81 season?

A) Aston Villa

B) Hamburg

C) Nottingham Forest

D) Real Madrid

225. Which teams did Liverpool beat en-route to the 1981 final of the European Cup?

A) Oulun Palloseura, Aberdeen, CSKA Sofia, Bayern Munich

B) Oulun Palloseura, Limerick, Honved, Internazionale

C) Spartak Moscow, Celtic, Levski Sofia, Hamburg

D) Spartak Moscow, Limerick, Honved, Bayern Munich

226. In which city was the 1981 European Cup final played?

A) London

B) Oslo

C) Paris

D) Rome

227. Who were Liverpool's opponents in the 1981 European Cup final?

A) Barcelona

B) Hamburg

C) Juventus

D) Real Madrid

228. Which British player lined up for Liverpool's opponents in the match?

A) Steve Archibald

B) Liam Brady

C) Laurie Cunningham

D) Kevin Keegan

229. What was the half-time score of the 1981 European Cup final?

A) 0-0

B) 1-0 to Liverpool

C) 0-1 to their opponents

D) 1-1

230. What was the final score of the 1981 European Cup final?

A) 1-0

B) 2-1

C) 3-1

D) 3-2

231. Who scored the winning goal of the 1981 European Cup final?

A) Kenny Dalglish

B) Alan Kennedy

C) Ray Kennedy

D) David Johnson

232. Who were Liverpool's joint-top scorers in the competition?

A) Kenny Dalglish and Ray Kennedy

B) Kenny Dalglish and Graeme Souness

C) Sammy Lee and David Johnson

D) Terry McDermott and Graeme Souness

2. TRIUMPHS AND DISASTERS

2A) THE RED MACHINE

Ian Rush

233. What is Ian Rush's date of birth?

A) 20th October 1956

B) 20th October 1961

C) 20th October 1966

D) 20th October 1971

234. What nationality is Rush?

A) Northern Irish

B) Irish

C) Scottish

D) Welsh

235. Who did Liverpool (first) sign Rush from?

A) Celtic

B) Chester

C) Shamrock Rovers

D) Everton

236. Which football club was Rush's favourite during childhood?

A) Celtic

B) Everton

C) Man U

D) Shamrock Rovers

237. In which year did Rush join Liverpool for the first time?

A) 1978

B) 1980

C) 1982

D) 1984

238. What was the transfer fee that Liverpool paid to sign Rush at that time?

A) £300,000

B) £500,000

C) £900,000

D) £1.1 million

239. How many (total) appearances did Rush make for Liverpool?

A) 440

B) 550

C) 660

D) 770

240. How many (total) goals did he score for Liverpool?

A) 269

B) 346

C) 399

D) 464

241. What is the highest number of goals Rush scored in a single league match for Liverpool?

A) 4

B) 5

C) 6

D) 7

242. In which year did the scoring feat occur?

A) 1980

B) 1983

C) 1986

D) 1989

243. Who were the opponents on the receiving end?

A) Grimsby Town

B) Luton Town

C) Mansfield Town

D) Northampton Town

244. For how many seasons was Rush the top goalscorer at Liverpool?

A) 4

B) 6

C) 8

D) 10

245. Between which years did Rush play for Juventus?

A) 1986 and 1987

B) 1987 and 1988

C) 1986 and 1988

D) 1987 and 1989

246. How many goals did Rush score for the Italian club?

A) 8

B) 18

C) 28

D) 38

247. In which year did Rush leave Liverpool for the final time as a player?

A) 1994

B) 1996

C) 1998

D) 2000

248. Which club did he join?

A) Everton

B) Leeds

C) Sunderland

D) Spurs

249. How many (total) games did he play for that club?

A) 43

B) 63

C) 83

D) 103

250. How many (total) goals did he score for them?

A) 3

B) 33

C) 63

D) 93

251. What were Rush's main playing attributes?

A) Combative, aggressive tackler, hard working, capable of getting forward and playing in advanced positions, playmaking, intelligence, ability to dictate tempo of games, low centre of gravity, great balance, vision, strong mentality, efficient distributor of the ball

B) A flamboyant, eccentric genius. Able to create goalscoring chances out of nothing. Scorer of great goals, often coming at the end of long, mazy dribbles

C) A hard-running player able to man-mark players out of the game, and whip in crosses that were unerringly accurate

D) Work-rate, closing down defenders, pace, goal-scoring instinct, clinical finisher, strength

1983-84 European Cup

252. Who were the defending champions in the 1983-84 European Cup?

A) Aston Villa

B) Hamburg

C) Juventus

D) Nottingham Forest

253. Who did Liverpool beat en-route to the 1984 European Cup final?

A) Gothenburg, Athletic Bilbao, Dundee United, Benfica

B) Gothenburg, CSKA Sofia, Dundee United, Dinamo Berlin

C) Odense, Athletic Bilbao, Benfica, Dinamo Bucharest

D) Odense, CSKA Sofia, Benfica, Dinamo Berlin

254. Where was the 1984 European Cup final played?

A) Olympic Stadium, Athens

B) Olympiastadion, Munich

C) Stadio Olimpico, Rome

D) Olympiastadion, Berlin

255. Who were Liverpool's opponents in the 1984 European Cup final?

A) Bayern Munich

B) Juventus

C) Panathinaikos

D) Roma

256. What was the half-time score in the 1984 European Cup final?

A) 0-0

B) 1-0 to Liverpool

C) 1-0 to Liverpool's opponents

D) 1-1

257. What was the score after 90 minutes?

A) 0-0

B) 1-1

C) 2-2

D) 3-3

258. What was the score in the penalty shoot-out at the end of the 1984 European Cup final?

A) 3-1

B) 4-2

C) 5-3

D) 6-5

259. Who was Liverpool's goalkeeper in the 1984 European Cup final?

A) Ray Clemence

B) Bruce Grobbelaar

C) Mike Hooper

D) Neville Southall

260. What antics did he get up to on the line to distract the penalty takers?

A) Doing a pull up on the crossbar as the players were preparing to take the penalty

B) Making the player wait by claiming his laces were undone

C) Pretending his legs were wobbling

D) Pulling funny faces

261. Who was Liverpool's top-scorer in the 1983-84 European Cup with five goals?

A) Kenny Dalglish

B) Phil Neal

C) Ian Rush

D) John Wark

1985-86 First Division

262. Liverpool's capture of the league title in 1986 meant that the Reds had been crowned Champions of England how many times?

A) 15

B) 16

C) 17

D) 18

263. Which had been the most recent year in which Liverpool had won the league title before they won it in 1986?

A) 1982

B) 1983

C) 1984

D) 1985

264. Which team finished runners-up to Liverpool in the First Division in 1986?

A) Everton

B) Man U

C) Nottingham Forest

D) West Ham

265. Who was Liverpool's leading goal scorer during the 1985-86 season?

A) Kenny Dalglish

B) Craig Johnston

C) Ian Rush

D) John Wark

266. Who played in every game of Liverpool's 1985-86 season?

A) Ray Clemence

B) Bruce Grobbelaar

C) Alan Hansen

D) Craig Johnston

267. What was the last major trophy Liverpool had won before they won the league in 1986?

A) European Cup

B) UEFA Cup

C) FA Cup

D) League Cup

1986 FA Cup

268. Who did Liverpool beat en-route to the 1986 FA Cup final against Everton?

A) Birmingham City, Manchester City, Coventry City, Sheffield United, Luton Town,

B) Birmingham City, Manchester City, York City, Spurs, Sheffield Wednesday

C) Exeter City, Blackburn Rovers, Spurs, Luton Town, Sheffield Wednesday

D) Norwich City, Chelsea, York City, Watford, Southampton

269. What was the half-time score in the 1986 FA Cup final?

A) 0-0

B) 0-1 to Everton

C) 1-0 to Liverpool

D) 2-1 to Liverpool

270. What was the full-time score of the 1986 FA Cup final?

A) 2-1 to Liverpool

B) 3-1 to Liverpool

C) 3-2 to Liverpool

D) 4-1 to Liverpool

271. Who scored Liverpool's first goal in the 1986 FA Cup final?

A) Kenny Dalglish

B) Craig Johnston

C) Ian Rush

D) Ronnie Whelan

272. Who scored Liverpool's last goal in the 1986 FA Cup final?

A) Kenny Dalglish

B) Craig Johnston

C) Ian Rush

D) Ronnie Whelan

273. Who scored for Everton in the 1986 FA Cup final?

A) Adrian Heath

B) Gary Lineker

C) Graeme Sharp

D) Trevor Steven

274. Who was the Everton manager in the 1986 FA Cup final?

A) Colin Harvey

B) Howard Kendall

C) Joe Royle

D) Mike Walker

275. How many English players were in the Liverpool starting 11?

A) 0

B) 3

C) 6

D) 9

276. How many English players were in Everton's starting 11?

A) 0

B) 2

C) 4

D) 7

John Barnes

277. What is John Barnes's date of birth?

A) 7th November 1959

B) 7th November 1963

C) 7th November 1967

D) 7th November 1971

278. What nationality is Barnes?

A) English

B) Irish

C) Jamaican

D) Welsh

279. Who was John Barnes named after?

A) John Charles

B) John F Kennedy

C) John Lennon

D) St John the Baptist

280. In which year did Barnes join Liverpool?

A) 1983

B) 1985

C) 1987

D) 1989

281. Who did Liverpool sign Barnes from?

A) Bradford City

B) Brentford

C) Celtic

D) Watford

282.What was the transfer fee that Liverpool paid to sign John Barnes?

A) £900,000

B) £1,900,000

C) £2,900,000

D) £3,900,000

283. Which player was Barnes's hero while growing up?

A) George Best

B) Johan Cruyff

C) Diego Maradona

D) Pele

284. Which club did Barnes end his playing career with?

A) Celtic

B) Charlton

C) Leeds

D) Newcastle

285. How many times was Barnes named PFA Player of the Year

A) 1

B) 2

C) 3

D) 4

286. What did Barnes injure in 1992 that dulled his acceleration?

A) Achilles Tendon

B) Ankle

C) Groin

D) Hamstring

287. How many international appearances did Barnes make?

A) 59

B) 69

C) 79

D) 89

288. How many international goals did Barnes score?

A) 11

B) 21

C) 31

D) 41

289. How many games did he play for Liverpool in total?

A) 203

B) 303

C) 403

D) 503

290. How many goals did he score for Liverpool in total?

A) 89

B) 106

C) 126

D) 149

291. How many goals did John Barnes score at Anfield for Liverpool?

A) 46

B) 58

C) 70

D) 82

292. What did John Barnes say after Everton fans threw bananas at him during a match?

A) "It's an absolute disgrace. As far as I am concerned, Everton are the biggest monkeys in the world"

B) "Some fruit and vegetable dealers did very well"

C) "Some monkeys seem to have been let out of the zoo today and came to the match"

D) "These so-called fans should be lined up and shot"

293. What was the name of the England World Cup 1990 song that Barnes rapped on?

A) "Coming Home"

B) "Football Delight"

C) "This Time We'll Get It Right"

D) "World in Motion"

294. What were John Barnes's playing attributes?

A) Aggressive, highly competitive central midfielder with a propensity to score great long strikes as a result of his phenomenally powerful shooting ability

B) Ball-playing defender who could pass the ball with both feet as well as make use use of explosive pace

C) Hard working full-back who was a dead ball specialist. Famous for scoring many of the greatest free kick goals the world has seen

D) Strength, skill, elegance, dribbling, balance, flair, crossing, vision

1989 FA Cup

295. During which round of the 1988-89 FA Cup did the Hillsborough Disaster occur?

A) Fourth

B) Fifth

C) Quarter-finals

D) Semi-finals

296. Who did Liverpool beat on the way to the 1989 FA Cup final?

A) Carlisle United, Millwall, Hull City, Brentford, Nottingham Forest

B) Carlisle United, Sheffield Wednesday, Plymouth, Wimbledon, Norwich

C) West Brom, Carlisle United, Sheffield Wednesday, Barnsley, Hull City

D) West From, Plymouth, Barnsley, Sheffield Wednesday, Norwich

297. Who did Liverpool face in the 1989 FA Cup final?

A) Arsenal

B) Everton

C) Man U

D) Nottingham Forest

298. What was the score at half-time in the 1989 FA Cup final?

A) 1-0 (to Liverpool)

B) 0-1 (to the opposition)

C) 1-1

D) 2-1

299. What was the score after 90 minutes in the 1989 FA Cup final?

A) 1-1

B) 2-2

C) 2-1

D) 3-2

300. Who captained Liverpool in the 1989 FA Cup final?

A) Kenny Dalglish

B) Alan Hansen

C) Steve McMahon

D) Ronnie Whelan

301. Who scored Liverpool's goals in the 1989 FA Cup final?

A) Aldridge and Rush

B) Barnes and Beardsley

C) McMahon and Houghton

D) Hansen and Whelan

302. Who scored for Liverpool's opponents in the 1989 FA Cup final?

A) Nigel Clough

B) Peter Davenport

C) Stuart McCall

D) Charlie Nicholas

303. How many Irishmen were in the Liverpool starting 11 for the 1989 FA Cup final?

A) 0

B) 2

C) 4

D) 7

304. How many Irishmen were in their opponents' starting 11?

A) 0

B) 1

C) 3

D) 5

305. How many Englishmen were in the Liverpool starting 11?

A) 0

B) 2

C) 4

D) 7

306. How many Englishmen were in Liverpool's opponent's starting 11?

A) 0

B) 1

C) 3

D) 5

The Eighties

307. In which country did the Heysel Stadium Disaster occur?

A) Belgium

B) France

C) Netherlands

D) Romania

308. How much did Juventus pay to sign Ian Rush in 1987?

A) £2.4 million

B) £2.8 million

C) £3.2 million

D) £3.6 million

309. After Ian Rush left to join Juventus in the summer of 1987, which three players joined Liverpool before the start of the 1987-88 season?

A) John Aldridge, John Barnes, Peter Beardsley

B) John Aldridge, John Barnes, Dean Saunders

C) John Barnes, Steve McMahon, Ray Houghton

D) Peter Beardsley, Ray Houghton, Nigel Spackman

310. Who was Liverpool's record transfer signing of the 1980s?

A) John Barnes

B) Peter Beardsley

C) Ian Rush

D) Dean Saunders

311. Which player joined Liverpool from Ajax in 1984?

A) Jan Molby

B) Jesper Olsen

C) Frank Rijkaard

D) Marco Van Basten

1989-90 First Division

312. Who finished second to Liverpool in the First Division in 1989-90?

A) Arsenal

B) Aston Villa

C) Spurs

D) West Ham

313. What was the points difference between first and second place at the end of the 1989-90 First Division season?

A) 3

B) 6

C) 9

D) 12

314. Which two players played in every Liverpool league game in 1989-90?

A) Ray Clemence and Barry Venison

B) Bruce Grobbelaar and Steve McMahon

C) Bruce Grobbelaar and Ian Rush

D) Steve McMahon and Ronnie Whelan

315. The 1989-90 First Division title meant that Liverpool had been crowned Champions of England how many times?

A) 16

B) 17

C) 18

D) 19

316. What was Liverpool's biggest league win of the 1989-90 season?

A) 8-1

B) 9-0

C) 10-0

D) 10-1

317. Who were Liverpool's opponents for that match?

A) Crystal Palace

B) Everton

C) Manchester City

D) Nottingham Forest

318. Who was Liverpool's leading goalscorer in 1989-90?

A) John Aldridge

B) John Barnes

C) Robbie Fowler

D) Ian Rush

The Nineties

319. Which player joined Liverpool in 1991, two years after scoring a last gasp goal at Anfield that won the league title for Arsenal?

A) Paul Merson

B) David Rocastle

C) Alan Smith

D) Michael Thomas

320. Who was Liverpool's record signing of the 1990s?

A) Stan Collymore

B) Emile Heskey

C) Paul Ince

D) Michael Owen

321. In which year was he signed?

A) 1993

B) 1995

C) 1997

D) 1999

322. What was the transfer fee that Liverpool paid for their most expensive signing of the 1990s?

A) £5.5 million

B) £8.5 million

C) £12 million

D) £15 million

323. Who said this?

"They compare Steve McManaman to Steve Heighway and he's nothing like him, but I can see why - it's because he's a bit different."

A) Peter Beardsley

B) Kevin Keegan

C) Ian Rush

D) Graeme Souness

324. Which of the following managers was in charge of Liverpool for the most games?

A) Rafa Benitez

B) Roy Evans

C) Gerard Houllier

D) Brendan Rodgers

1992 FA Cup

325. Who did Liverpool beat en-route to the 1992 FA Cup final?

A) Crewe Alexandra, Bristol Rovers, Ipswich Town, Aston Villa, Portsmouth

B) Crewe Alexandra, Oxford United, West Ham United, Aston Villa, Norwich

C) Port Vale, Bristol Rovers, Ipswich Town, Chelsea, Portsmouth

D) Port Vale, Oxford United, West Ham United, Chelsea, Norwich

326. Who were the defending FA Cup holders in 1991-92?

A) Arsenal

B) Man U

C) Nottingham Forest

D) Spurs

327. Who did Liverpool face in the 1992 FA Cup final?

A) Man U

B) Middlesbrough

C) Newcastle

D) Sunderland

328. Who was Liverpool's captain in the 1992 FA Cup final?

A) Alan Hansen

B) Jan Molby

C) Ronnie Whelan

D) Mark Wright

329. What was the half-time score in the 1992 FA Cup final?

A) 0-0

B) 1-0 to Liverpool

C) 1-0 to their opponents

D) 1-1

330. What was the final score of the 1992 FA Cup final?

A) 2-0

B) 2-1

C) 3-0

D) 3-1

331. Who scored first for Liverpool in the 1992 FA Cup final?

A) Ray Houghton

B) Ian Rush

C) Dean Saunders

D) Michael Thomas

332. Who scored last for Liverpool in the 1992 FA Cup final?

A) Ray Houghton

B) Ian Rush

C) Dean Saunders

D) Michael Thomas

333. Why did the Liverpool manager miss the 1992 FA Cup semi-final?

A) He had resigned from the club (only to be later persuaded to stay by the board)

B) He had a severe stomach upset on the day of the game

C) He was banned from the touchline for swearing at a linesman

D) He was recovering from triple heart bypass surgery

334. Who took charge of managerial duties in his absence?

A) Kenny Dalglish and Alan Hansen

B) Jan Molby and Ronnie Whelan

C) Ronnie Moran and Roy Evans

D) Ian Rush and John Barnes

Robbie Fowler

335. What is Fowler's full name?

A) Robbie Fowler

B) Robert Bernard Fowler

C) Robert Dennis Fowler

D) Robert Kenneth Fowler

336. What is Fowler's date of birth?

A) 9th April 1972

B) 9th April 1975

C) 9th April 1978

D) 9th April 1981

337. In which part of Liverpool was Fowler born?

A) Anfield

B) Croxteth

C) Huyton

D) Toxteth

338. In which year did Fowler make his Liverpool debut?

A) 1991

B) 1993

C) 1995

D) 1997

339. How many goals did Fowler score on his Liverpool debut?

A) 0

B) 1

C) 3

D) 5

340. How many games did Fowler play for Liverpool in total?

A) 230

B) 369

C) 430

D) 509

341. How many goals did Fowler score for Liverpool in total?

A) 183

B) 222

C) 275

D) 333

342. For how many seasons was Fowler the leading league goalscorer for Liverpool?

A) 3

B) 4

C) 5

D) 6

343. What was Fowler's nickname at Anfield?

A) Docker

B) God

C) Shaggy

D) Sniffer

344. What trophies did Liverpool win while Fowler was at the club?

A) 1 League title, 1 FA Cup, 1 League Cup, 1 UEFA Cup, 1 UEFA Super Cup

B) 2 FA Cups, 1 League Cup, 1 UEFA Cup, 1 UEFA Super Cup

C) 1 FA Cup, 2 League Cups, 1 UEFA Cup, 1 UEFA Super Cup

D) 1 League Cup, 1 UEFA Cup

345. How many England caps did Fowler win?

A) 18

B) 26

C) 42

D) 58

346. How many England goals did Fowler score?

A) 7

B) 14

C) 28

D) 35

347. How many competitive goals did Fowler score for England?

A) 1

B) 9

C) 15

D) 21

348. Who did Fowler leave Liverpool to join?

A) AC Milan

B) Leeds United

C) Manchester City

D) Real Madrid

349. In which year did Fowler leave Liverpool?

A) 1999

B) 2001

C) 2003

D) 2005

350. How many (total) games did Fowler play for the club he joined after leaving Liverpool?

A) 33

B) 63

C) 93

D) 123

351. How many (total) goals did Fowler score for the club he joined after leaving Liverpool?

A) 14

B) 28

C) 56

D) 112

352. Which country did Fowler end his professional playing career in?

A) Australia

B) Austria

C) Thailand

D) USA

353. What were Fowler's playing attributes?

A) Dynamism, discipline, energy, and ball-winning

B) Calmness, composure, spraying the ball around from midfield areas with effortless ease

C) Tough-tackling, unflinching, uncompromising central defender

D) Quickness and opportunism in goal-scoring areas, accurate and powerful shot, good in the air, goal-scorer and good team-player

The 2000s

354. Who was Liverpool's record signing of the 2000s?

A) Andy Carroll

B) Djibril Cisse

C) Emile Heskey

D) Fernando Torres

355. Which club did Liverpool's record signing of the 2000s join from?

A) Atletico Madrid

B) Auxerre

C) Leicester

D) Newcastle

356. What was the transfer fee that Liverpool paid for their record signing of the 2000s?

A) £10 million

B) £26.5 million

C) £35 million

D) £50 million

357. How many appearances did Liverpool's record signing of the 2000s make for the club?

A) 102

B) 142

C) 182

D) 222

358. How many goals did he score for Liverpool?

A) 65

B) 81

C) 96

D) 110

Michael Owen

359. Where was Michael Owen born?

A) Chester

B) Chesterfield

C) Mansfield

D) Manchester

360. What is Owen's date of birth?

A) 14th December 1976

B) 14th December 1979

C) 14th December 1982

D) 14th December 1985

361. Who wrote a personal letter to Owen which convinced him to sign a schoolboy contract with Liverpool?

A) Steve Heighway

B) Ben Kingsley

C) Prince Philip

D) Graeme Souness

362. How many games did Owen play for Liverpool in total?

A) 216

B) 297

C) 378

D) 469

363. How many goals did he score for Liverpool in total?

A) 158

B) 198

C) 238

D) 278

364. Apart from Liverpool, which are the other clubs that Owen played for?

A) Barcelona, Middlesborough, Leeds United, Everton

B) Barcelona, Newcastle United, Chelsea, Sunderland

C) Real Madrid, Newcastle United, Manchester United, Stoke City

D) Real Madrid, Sunderland, Manchester City, Southampton

365. How many games did Owen play for England?

A) 58

B) 65

C) 77

D) 89

366. How many goals did Owen score for England?

A) 30

B) 40

C) 60

D) 80

367. What pursuit did Owen take up after retiring from playing football?

A) Ballroom dancing

B) Banger racing driver

C) Racehorse breeding and owning

D) Showjumping jockey

368. What did Owen win during his playing career?

A) 2 English League titles, 2 FA Cups, 3 League Cups, 2 FA Community Shields, 1 Champions League, 1 UEFA Cup, 1 UEFA Super Cup

B) 1 English League title, 1 FA Cup, 3 League Cups, 2 FA Community Shields, 1 UEFA Cup, 1 UEFA Super Cup, 1 Ballon D'Or, 1 World Soccer World Player of the Year Award

C) 1 English League title, 1 Spanish League Title, 1 FA Cup, 2 League Cups, 2 FA Community Shields, 1 Champions League, 1 UEFA Cup, 1 UEFA Super Cup, 1 Ballon D'Or, 1 World Soccer World Player of the Year Award

D) FA Cup, 3 League Cups, 2 FA Community Shields, 1 Champions League, 1 UEFA Cup, 1 UEFA Super Cup, 1 Ballon D'Or

369. What were Owen's main playing attributes?

A) Amazing leadership quality, inspirational captain, strong competitor, physically imposing central defender

B) Hard-working defensive central midfielder, energetic, stamina, good all-round ability

C) Passing ability, style, flamboyance, technique, skill, exquisite touch

D) Prolific goal-scoring ability, pace, vision, awareness

370. What height is Michael Owen?

A) 5’7

B) 5’8

C) 5’9

D) 5’10

Steven Gerrard

371. What is Steven Gerrard’s middle name?

A) Andrew

B) George

C) Patrick

D) Matthew

372. In which year was Gerrard born?

A) 1978

B) 1980

C) 1982

D) 1984

373. What height is Steven Gerrard?

A) 5’9

B) 5’10

C) 5’11

D) 6’

374. How many total appearances did Gerrard make for Liverpool?

A) 390

B) 470

C) 550

D) 710

375. How many goals did he score for Liverpool in total?

A) 96

B) 142

C) 186

D) 217

376. How many England caps does Gerrard have?

A) 84

B) 94

C) 104

D) 114

377. How many goals did Gerrard score for England?

A) 21

B) 29

C) 41

D) 47

378. In which year did Gerrard join Liverpool?

A) 1994

B) 1996

C) 1998

D) 2000

379. Who were Gerrard's childhood heroes?

A) John Barnes, Ian Rush, and Paul Gascoigne

B) Peter Beardsley, John Aldridge, and Gary Lineker

C) Steve McMahon, Jan Molby, and Alan Shearer

D) Ronnie Whelan, Craig Johnston, and Glenn Hoddle

380. In which year did Gerrard make his first team debut?

A) 1995

B) 1996

C) 1997

D) 1998

381. In which year did he make his final appearance for Liverpool?

A) 2014

B) 2015

C) 2016

D) 2017

382. Which club did Gerrard join after leaving Liverpool?

A) Chelsea

B) Glasgow Rangers

C) LA Galaxy

D) Real Madrid

383. How many total games did Gerrard play for his new club?

A) 38

B) 58

C) 78

D) 98

384. Which club did Gerrard join as manager in 2018?

A) Bolton Wanderers

B) Glasgow Rangers

C) LA Galaxy

D) Queens Park Rangers

385. Which player, according to Gerrard, was too good to play for Arsenal?

A) Himself

B) Dennis Bergkamp

C) Thierry Henry

D) Luis Suarez

386. What were Gerrard's playing attributes?

A) Attacking full back with an eye for goal

B) A prolific goalscorer who could shoot with power and accuracy with both feet as well as score with his head. Gifted with pace, physicality and stamina

C) Tricky winger who used pace and power to bomb forward at every available opportunity. Master of the banana free-kick that would curl wickedly and find its way past the keeper into the net

D) Versatile, hard-working, box-to-box midfielder, ability to make late runs, and score goals from distance, technical skills, aerial ability, defensive skills, leadership, determination, influence on the pitch

Jamie Carragher

387. What is Carragher's full name?

A) James Francis Dixie Carragher

B) James Lee Duncan Carragher

C) James Ronald Rudolph Carragher

D) James William Kenneth Carragher

388. What is his date of birth?

A) 24th January 1974

B) 26th January 1976

C) 28th January 1978

D) 30th January 1980

389. What is his height?

A) 5’11

B) 6’

C) 6’1

D) 6’2

390. Which was the boyhood club of Carragher?

A) Aston Villa

B) Everton

C) Liverpool

D) Nottingham Forest

391. How many clubs did Carragher play for during his career?

A) 1

B) 2

C) 3

D) 4

392. How many games did Carragher play for Liverpool in total?

A) 637

B) 737

C) 837

D) 919

393. How many games did Carragher play for England?

A) 38

B) 58

C) 78

D) 84

394. What title did he give to his autobiography?

A) Carra: My Autobiography

B) Carra's Way

C) My Life by Carra

D) This is Carra's Life

395. What did he win with Liverpool?

A) 1 FA Youth Cup, 1 League title, 3 League Cups, 2 Community Shields, 1 Champions League, 1 UEFA Super Cup

B) 1 FA Youth Cup, 2 FA Cups, 3 League Cups, 2 Community Shields, 1 Champions League, 1 UEFA Cup, 2 UEFA Super Cups

C) 1 FA Youth Cup, 1 FA Cup, 2 League Cups, 2 Community Shields, 1 Champions League, 1 UEFA Cup

D) 1 FA Youth Cup, 1 League title, 1 FA Cup, 1 League Cup, 2 Community Shields, 1 Champions League, 1 UEFA Cup, 1 UEFA Super Cup

396. What shirt number did Jamie Carragher wear for Liverpool?

A) 4

B) 5

C) 14

D) 23

397. For how many years did he play for the club?

A) 11

B) 14

C) 17

D) 20

398. What were Carragher's playing attributes?

A) Defending from a midfield position, passing, tackling, dictating the tempo of the game

B) Dribbling, trickery, skill

C) Goal poacher extraordinaire, knack of being in exactly at the right place at the right time to maintain a prolific scoring rate

D) Strength, tackling, consistent, organisational ability, tactical awareness

2B) ABSOLUTE ENTERTAINMENT

2001 FA Cup

399. Who did Liverpool beat en-route to the 2001 FA Cup final?

A) Cardiff, Bolton Wanderers, Blackburn Rovers, Leeds United, Spurs

B) Carlisle United, QPR, Chelsea, Blackburn Rovers, Spurs

C) Rotherham, Leeds, Manchester City, Tranmere Rovers, Wycombe Wanderers

D) Wycombe Wanderers, Leeds, QPR, Blackburn Rovers, Manchester City

400. In which city was the 2001 FA Cup final played?

A) Birmingham

B) Cardiff

C) Ipswich

D) London

401. Who were Liverpool's opponents in the 2001 FA Cup final?

A) Arsenal

B) Everton

C) Man City

D) Man U

402. What was the half-time score in the 2001 FA Cup final?

A) 0-0

B) 1-1

C) 1-0 to Liverpool

D) 0-1 to their opponents

403. What was the score after 90 minutes?

A) 1-0

B) 1-1

C) 2-1

D) 3-1

404. Who scored for Liverpool in the 2001 FA Cup final?

A) Robbie Fowler

B) Steven Gerrard

C) Emile Heskey

D) Michael Owen

405. What was Liverpool's trophy haul for the year 2001?

A) League title, FA Cup, UEFA Cup, Charity Shield

B) League title, FA Cup, Charity Shield

C) League Cup, FA Cup, UEFA Cup, UEFA Super Cup, Charity Shield

D) League Cup, FA Cup, UEFA Cup, Charity Shield

406. Who was the manager of Liverpool's opponents in the 2001 FA Cup final?

A) Alex Ferguson

B) Joe Royle

C) Walter Smith

D) Arsene Wenger

407. Which two Germans were in the Liverpool starting line-up for the 2001 FA Cup final?

A) Markus Babbel, Dietmar Hamman

B) Markus Babbel, Karl-Heinz Reidle

C) Lothar Matthaus, Thomas Linke

D) Karl-Heinz Reidle, Christian Ziege

408. Who was Liverpool's goalkeeper in the 2001 FA Cup final?

A) Scott Carson

B) David James

C) Pepe Reina

D) Sander Westerveld

409. Who was the man of the match in the 2001 FA Cup final?

A) Robbie Fowler

B) Steven Gerrard

C) Emile Heskey

D) Michael Owen

2001 League Cup

410. Who did Liverpool beat en-route to the 2001 League Cup final?

A) Brentford, Stoke, Cardiff, West Ham

B) Bristol Rovers, Stoke, Man U, Swansea

C) Chelsea, Stoke, Fulham, Crystal Palace

D) Fulham, Stoke, Brighton, Swansea

411. Who did Liverpool face in the 2001 League Cup final?

A) Aston Villa

B) Birmingham City

C) Derby County

D) Leicester City

412. In which city was the 2001 League Cup final played?

A) Birmingham

B) Cardiff

C) London

D) Swansea

413. By what scoreline did Liverpool win their second tie of the tournament?

A) 5-0

B) 6-0

C) 0-7

D) 0-8

414. What was the half-time score in the 2001 League Cup final?

A) 0-0

B) 1-0 to Liverpool

C) 0-1 to their opponents

D) 1-1

415. What was the 2001 League Cup final score after 90 minutes?

A) 0-0

B) 1-1

C) 2-2

D) 3-3

416. What was the score after extra-time?

A) 0-0

B) 1-1

C) 2-2

D) 3-3

417. What was the score of the penalty shoot-out?

A) 3-1

B) 4-2

C) 5-4

D) 6-5

418. Who missed their penalty for Liverpool in the penalty shoot-out?

A) Hamann

B) McAllister

C) Barmby

D) Ziege

419. Who scored Liverpool's last penalty?

A) Carragher

B) Fowler

C) Hamann

D) McAllister

420. Who missed the last penalty for their opponents?

A) Geoff Horsfield

B) Andrew Johnson

C) Stan Lazaridis

D) Marcelo

421. The victory meant that Liverpool had won the League Cup how many times?

A) 5

B) 6

C) 7

D) 8

422. As of 2020, how many League Cups have Liverpool won?

A) 5

B) 6

C) 7

D) 8

2000-01 UEFA Cup

423. Who were the reigning champions in the 2000-01 UEFA Cup?

A) Arsenal

B) Galatasary

C) Leeds

D) Parma

424. Who did Liverpool beat en-route to the 2000-01 UEFA Cup final?

A) Fenerbahce, Lillestrom, Roma, Benfica, Real Madrid, Borussia Dortmund

B) Galatasaray, Slovan Bratislava, Rosenborg, Roma, Porto, Barcelona

C) Gaziantepspor, Lillestrom, Rosenborg, Inter Milan, Rayo Vallecano, Kaiserslautern

D) Rapid Bucharest, Slovan Liberec, Olympiakos, Roma, Porto, Barcelona

425. In which city was the 2001 UEFA Cup final played?

A) Dortmund

B) Seville

C) Vienna

D) Zurich

426. Who were Liverpool's opponents in the 2001 UEFA Cup final?

A) Alaves

B) Atalanta

C) Borussia Dortmund

D) Udinese

427. What was the score at half-time of the 2001 UEFA Cup final?

A) 0-0

B) 1-1

C) 2-1 to Liverpool

D) 3-1 to Liverpool

428. What was the score after 90 minutes of the 2001 UEFA Cup final?

A) 2-2

B) 3-3

C) 4-4

D) 5-5

429. What was the final score of the 2001 UEFA Cup final?

A) 3-2 to Liverpool

B) 4-2 to Liverpool

C) 4-3 to Liverpool

D) 5-4 to Liverpool

430.Who didn't score for Liverpool in the 2001 UEFA Cup final?

A) Markus Babbel

B) Robbie Fowler

C) Steven Gerrard

D) Michael Owen

431. Who scored a penalty for Liverpool in the 2001 UEFA Cup final?

A) Robbie Fowler

B) Steven Gerrard

C) Gary McAllister

D) Michael Owen

432. Who was the 2001 UEFA Cup final man of the match?

A) Robbie Fowler

B) Steven Gerrard

C) Gary McAllister

D) Michael Owen

433. The victory meant that Liverpool had won the UEFA Cup how many times?

A) 3

B) 5

C) 7

D) 9

434. Victory also meant that Liverpool would go on to play which team for the 2001 UEFA Super Cup?

A) Atletico Madrid

B) Barcelona

C) Bayern Munich

D) Real Madrid

435. What was the score in that match?

A) 1-0 to Liverpool

B) 2-0 to Liverpool

C) 2-1 to Liverpool

D) 3-2 to Liverpool

436. What was Liverpool's final position in the Premier League in 2000-01?

A) 1st

B) 2nd

C) 3rd

D) 4th

Rafa Benitez

437. Which was the first team to be managed by Rafa Benitez?

A) Real Madrid

B) Real Madrid B

C) Real Valladolid

D) Valencia

438. Which club did Benitez manage immediately prior to joining Liverpool?

A) Athletic Bilbao

B) Real Madrid

C) Real Madrid B

D) Valencia

439. In which year did Benitez join Liverpool?

A) 2001

B) 2002

C) 2003

D) 2004

440. What major trophies did Benitez win with Liverpool?

A) FA Cup, Champions League, UEFA Super Cup

B) FA Cup, League title

C) Champions League, FA Cup, League Cup

D) League title, League Cup

441. Which of the following trophies has Benitez not won as a manager?

A) European Cup Winners' Cup

B) Europa League

C) Spanish Primera Division

D) FIFA Club World Cup

442. Which of the following clubs has Benitez not managed?

A) Extremadura

B) Mallorca

C) Osasuna

D) Tenerife

443. Which Chinese club did Benitez join in July 2019?

A) Dalian

B) Guangzhou

C) Shandong

D) Shanghai

444. How many professional sides had Benitez managed in Europe up to that point?

A) 8

B) 12

C) 16

D) 20

2004-05 Champions League

445. Who were the defending champions going into the 2004-05 Champions League tournament?

A) AC Milan

B) Barcelona

C) Porto

D) Real Madrid

446. Who did Liverpool beat en-route to the 2004-05 Champions League final?

A) Bayer Leverkusen, Internazionale, Chelsea

B) Bayer Leverkusen, Juventus, Chelsea

C) Man U, Bayern Munich, Ajax

D) Man U, Internazionale, PSV Eindhoven

447. In which city was the 2005 Champions League final played?

A) Copenhagen

B) Istanbul

C) Vienna

D) Zurich

448. Who did Liverpool's opponents, AC Milan, beat to reach the 2005 Champions League final?

A) Bayer Leverkusen, Internazionale, Chelsea

B) Bayer Leverkusen, Juventus, Chelsea

C) Man U, Ajax, Bayern Munich

D) Man U, Internazionale, PSV Eindhoven

449. Going into the 2005 Champions League final, how many times had AC Milan been crowned Champions of Europe?

A) 4

B) 6

C) 8

D) 10

450. What was the half-time score in the 2005 Champions League final?

A) 1-1

B) 3-0 to Liverpool

C) 0-2 to their opponents

D) 0-3 to their opponents

451. What was the score at full-time of the 2005 Champions League final?

A) 2-2

B) 3-3

C) 4-4

D) 5-5

452. Who didn't score for Liverpool in the 2005 Champions League final?

A) Xabi Alonso

B) Luis Garcia

C) Steven Gerrard

D) Vladimir Smicer

453. Who scored Liverpool's first goal in the match?

A) Xabi Alonso

B) Luis Garcia

C) Steven Gerrard

D) Vladimir Smicer

454. Who missed a penalty for Liverpool in the 2005 Champions League final?

A) Xabi Alonso

B) Djibril Cisse

C) John Arne Riise

D) Vladimir Smicer

455. Who missed Milan's last penalty?

A) Kaka

B) Andrea Pirlo

C) Serginho

D) Andrei Shevchenko

456. How many minutes did it take for Liverpool to score all of their goals in normal time of the 2005 Champions League final?

A) 6

B) 12

C) 18

D) 24

457. The victory meant that Liverpool had been crowned champions of Europe how many times?

A) 3

B) 5

C) 7

D) 9

2006 FA Cup

458. Who did Liverpool beat en-route to the 2006 FA Cup final?

A) Luton Town, Blackburn Rovers, Manchester City, Manchester United, Chelsea

B) Luton Town, Portsmouth, Manchester United, Birmingham City, Chelsea

C) Norwich City, Blackburn Rovers, Bolton Wanderers, Manchester City, Middlesbrough

D) Norwich City, Portsmouth, Bolton Wanderers, Birmingham City, Newcastle United

459. Who did Liverpool face in the 2006 FA Cup final?

A) Chelsea

B) Crystal Palace

C) Millwall

D) West Ham United

460. In which city was the 2006 FA Cup final played?

A) Birmingham

B) Cardiff

C) Carlisle

D) London

461. Which Liverpool player was the joint-top scorer in the tournament?

A) Peter Crouch

B) Robbie Fowler

C) Steven Gerrard

D) Fernando Torres

462. At which stadium did Liverpool pull off a remarkable victory in the quarter-finals of the 2005-06 FA Cup?

A) Anfield

B) City of Manchester Stadium

C) Old Trafford

D) St Andrews

463. What was Liverpool's quarter-final score?

A) 0-5

B) 0-7

C) 1-8

D) 9-0

464. What was the half-time score in the 2006 FA Cup final?

A) 0-0

B) 1-1

C) 2-1 to Liverpool

D) 1-2 to Liverpool's opponents

465. What was the 2006 FA Cup final score after 90 mins?

A) 0-0

B) 1-1

C) 2-2

D) 3-3

466. What was the score after extra-time?

A) 0-0

B) 1-1

C) 2-2

D) 3-3

467. At whose end were the penalties taken?

A) Liverpool

B) Neutral

C) Liverpool's opponents

D) Mixed support

468. What was the score of the penalty shootout?

A) 3-1

B) 4-2

C) 5-3

D) 6-5

469. Who didn't score in the penalty shootout?

A) Gerrard

B) Hamann

C) Hypia

D) Riise

470. The triumph, still Liverpool's most recent in the FA Cup (as of 2020) meant that Liverpool have won the world's oldest cup competition how many times?

A) 5

B) 7

C) 9

D) 11

3. ULTRA-MODERN LIVERPOOL

3A) NEW HEIGHTS OF GLORY

The 2010s

471. Who said going from London to Liverpool was more of a culture shock than going to France?

A) Nathaniel Clyne

B) Ashley Cole

C) Joe Cole

D) Raheem Sterling

472. About who did manager Brendan Rodgers say that "his skills were like Ricky Villa, but his finish was like Ricky Gervais"?

A) Iago Aspas

B) Andy Carroll

C) Lucas Leiva

D) Raheem Sterling

473. Which Liverpool player said this about his mother?

“She thinks she’s Jose Mourinho. Some of the stuff she’s telling me, the manager is telling me as well. She really knows about the game.”

A) Nathaniel Clyne

B) Steven Gerrard

C) Sadio Mane

D) Raheem Sterling

474. For which of the following players did Liverpool pay their record transfer fee (as of 2020)?

A) Andy Carroll

B) Sadio Mane

C) Mo Salah

D) Virgil van Dijk

475. For which player did Liverpool receive their biggest-ever transfer fee (as of 2020)?

A) Andy Carroll

B) Philippe Coutinho

C) Raheem Sterling

D) Luis Suarez

476. Which club did Liverpool sign Luis Suarez from in 2011?

A) Ajax

B) Benfica

C) Penarol

D) Sao Paolo

477. How much did Liverpool pay AC Milan to sign Mario Balotelli?

A) £16 million

B) £24 million

C) £32 million

D) £40 million

478. Liverpool signed three players from which club in the 2014 pre-season?

A) Borussia Dortmund

B) Hoffenheim

C) Red Bull Salzburg

D) Southampton

479. From which club did Roberto Firmino sign for Liverpool?

A) Borussia Dortmund

B) Hoffenheim

C) Red Bull Salzburg

D) Southampton

480. From which club did Liverpool sign Mo Salah?

A) Chelsea

B) Red Bull Salzburg

C) Roma

D) Zamalek

481. From which club did Liverpool sign Sadio Mane?

A) Hoffenheim

B) Red Bull Leipzig

C) Red Bull Salzburg

D) Southampton

482. From which club did Liverpool sign Virgil Van Dijk?

A) Celtic

B) Red Bull Salzburg

C) Southampton

D) Vitesse Arnhem

Luis Suarez

483. What is Suarez's date of birth?

A) 30th January 1985

B) 27th January 1986

C) 24th January 1987

D) 21st January 1988

484. What is Suarez's height?

A) 5'9

B) 5'10

C) 5'11

D) 6'

485. What is his nationality?

A) Argentinian

B) Peruvian

C) Spanish

D) Uruguayan

486. What unusual disciplinary issue has Suarez had on more than one occasion?

A) Biting players

B) Jumping into the crowd in an aggressive manner

C) Rugby tackling players

D) Swearing at referees

487. Who had Suarez not played for before joining Liverpool?

A) Ajax Amsterdam

B) Groningen

C) Nacional

D) Penarol

488. How much did Liverpool sign Suarez for?

A) £18.9 million

B) £22.8 million

C) £29 million

D) £33.8 million

489. Who signed for Liverpool on the same day as Suarez?

A) Andy Carroll

B) Raheem Sterling

C) Daniel Sturridge

D) Fernando Torres

490. How many games did Suarez play for Liverpool in total?

A) 133

B) 157

C) 181

D) 219

491. How many goals did Suarez score for Liverpool in total?

A) 82

B) 106

C) 130

D) 149

492. What was the transfer fee Barcelona paid Liverpool to sign Suarez?

A) £55 million

B) £65 million

C) £75 million

D) £85 million

493. What trophies did Liverpool win while Suarez was at the club?

A) League title

B) FA Cup and League Cup

C) League Cup

D) UEFA Cup

494. What individual awards did Suarez win while playing for Liverpool?

A) 3x Liverpool Player of the Season, 3x Liverpool Players' Player of the Season, PFA Players' Player of the Year, FWA Footballer of the Year x 2,Premier League Golden Boot, 2x European Golden Shoe

B) Liverpool Player of the Season x 2, Liverpool Players' Player of the Season, Liverpool Goal of the Season, PFA Players' Player of the Year, FWA Footballer of the Year, Premier League Player of the Season, Premier League Golden Boot, European Golden Shoe

C) Liverpool Player of the Season x 2, Liverpool Players' Player of the Season, Liverpool Goal of the Season, PFA Players' Player of the Year, FWA Footballer of the Year, Premier League Player of the Season, Ballon D'Or

D) Liverpool Player of the Season, Liverpool Players' Player of the Season, Liverpool Goal of the Season, PFA Players' Player of the Year, FWA Footballer of the Year x 2, Premier League Golden Boot, European Golden Shoe

495. What had he won after his first 18 months at Barcelona?

A) Nothing

B) 1 Copa del Rey

C) 1 Spanish Primera title, 1 Copa del Rey

D) 1 Spanish Primera title, 1 Copa del Rey, 1 Champions League, 1 UEFA Super Cup, 1 FIFA Club World Cup

496. Which club did Suarez leave Barcelona to join?

A) Arsenal

B) Atletico Madrid

C) Real Madrid

D) Sevilla

497. What were Suarez's playing attributes for Liverpool?

A) Attacking from the left-back position, defending, marking, goal-line clearances

B) Defending from a midfield position, passing, tackling, dictating the tempo of the game

C) Highly competitive central midfielder with excellent passing ability

D) Shooting, dribbling, work-rate, aggression, intelligence, pace

Jurgen Klopp

498. What is Jurgen Klopp's middle name?

A) Nolberto

B) Norbert

C) Robert

D) Reinhard

499. Which part of Germany is Klopp from?

A) Black Forest

B) Blue Forest

C) Green Forest

D) Red Forest

500. With which club did Jurgen Klopp spend the vast majority of his playing career?

A) Bayer Leverkusen

B) Borussia Dortmund

C) Eintracht Frankfurt

D) Mainz 05

501. Which clubs did Klopp manage before joining Liverpool?

A) Bayer Leverkusen, Bayern Munich

B) Eintracht Frankfurt, Mainz 05

C) Eintracht Frankfurt, Borussia Dortmund

D) Mainz 05, Borussia Dortmund

502. In which year did Klopp join Liverpool?

A) 2013

B) 2014

C) 2015

D) 2016

503. During his first press conference, Klopp described himself as .... ?

A) "The Good One"

B) "The Great One"

C) "The Normal One"

D) "The Wonderful One"

504. What is the name of the footballing philosophy that Klopp is said to have popularised?

A) Gegen-plex

B) Gegen-press

C) Goggle-press

D) Google-plex

505. Which legendary manager does Klopp cite as one of his major influences?

A) Marcelo Bielsa

B) Viktor Maslov

C) Rinus Michels

D) Arrigo Sacchi

Mo Salah

506. What is Salah's date of birth?

A) 15th June 1990

B) 15th June 1992

C) 15th September 1994

D) 15th December 1996

507. What is Salah's height?

A) 5’7

B) 5’9

C) 5’11

D) 6’1

508. Near which city was Salah born?

A) Baghdad

B) Basra

C) Basyoun

D) Cairo

509. Which club did Salah join in 2012?

A) Al Mokawloon

B) Basel

C) Red Bull Salzburg

D) Zamalek

510. Which was Salah’s first English club?

A) Arsenal

B) Chelsea

C) Everton

D) Peterborough United

511. How many games did Salah play for them in total?

A) 19

B) 39

C) 59

D) 79

512. How many goals did he score for them in total?

A) 2

B) 22

C) 42

D) 62

513. Which Italian team did Liverpool sign Salah from?

A) Brescia

B) Juventus

C) Roma

D) Udinese

514. What was the transfer fee that Liverpool paid to sign Salah?

A) £30.6 million

B) £33.9 million

C) £36.9 million

D) £39.6 million

515. How many total goals did Salah score for Liverpool in his debut season?

A) 24

B) 34

C) 44

D) 54

516. Who has scored more goals than Salah in their first 100 Premier League appearances for a single team?

A) Sergio Aguero

B) Alan Shearer

C) Fernando Torres

D) Ruud van Nistelrooy

517. What are Salah's main playing attributes?

A) Fearless competitor, physically imposing central defender

B) Hard-working defensive central midfielder, energetic, stamina, good all-round ability

C) Leadership, dominant in the air. Outstanding positioning, ability to read the game, ability to dictate play with the ball at his feet, technically brilliant, intelligent, two footed

D) Quickness, mobility, hard-working, technique, touch, clinical finishing, dribbling

Sadio Mane

518. What is Mane's date of birth?

A) 10th January 1991

B) 10th April 1992

C) 10th October 1993

D) 10th December 1994

519. What is his height?

A) 5'9

B) 5'10

C) 5'11

D) 6'

520. What nationality is Sadio Mane?

A) Austrian

B) French

C) Senegalese

D) Swiss

521. Which club did he join in 2011?

A) Mainz 05

B) Metz

C) Red Bull Leipzig

D) Red Bull Salzburg

522. Which was Mane's first English club?

A) Aldershot

B) Arsenal

C) Bournemouth

D) Southampton

523. How many games did he play for them in total?

A) 7

B) 75

C) 125

D) 175

524. How many goals did he score for them in total?

A) 2

B) 25

C) 50

D) 100

525. Which team did Liverpool sign Mane from?

A) Bournemouth

B) Metz

C) Red Bull Salzburg

D) Southampton

526. How many total goals did he score for Liverpool in his debut season?

A) 13

B) 23

C) 43

D) 53

527. In which year did Mane win his first African Player of the Year Award?

A) 2017

B) 2018

C) 2019

D) 2020

528. What are Mane's main playing attributes?

A) A super-sub with an assassin's instinct. Goal-poacher extraordinaire. A classic number nine. Physical and dominant. Ability to hang in the air like a salmon and head the ball brilliantly. Can change games by studying the opposition while on the bench and exploiting weak spots

B) Intensity, concentration, two-footed, heading ability, explosive pace, prolific goalscoring, trickery, tactical awareness, creativity, agility, balance, touch, passing, psychological strength

C) Hard-running midfielder. Elegant tackler. Wonderful crosser of the ball

D) Master of retaining possession through quick, short passes

Virgil van Dijk

529. What nationality is Virgil?

A) Dutch

B) German

C) South African

D) Zimbabwean

530. What is his height?

A) 6'2

B) 6'3

C) 6'4

D) 6'5

531. Which club did he join in 2011?

A) Celtic

B) Groningen

C) PSV Eindhoven

D) Southampton

532. Which was Virgil's first English club?

A) Arsenal

B) Bournemouth

C) Grimsby Town

D) Southampton

533. How many games did he play for them in total?

A) 80

B) 100

C) 120

D) 140

534. How many goals did he score for them?

A) 7

B) 10

C) 14

D) 21

535. Which team did Liverpool sign him from?

A) Bournemouth

B) Celtic

C) PSV Eindhoven

D) Southampton

536. What had the teams that Virgil was a part of won before he joined Liverpool?

A) 2 Scottish Premierships, 1 Scottish League Cup

B) 1 Scottish Premiership, 1 Scottish Cup, 1 Scottish League Cup

C) 1 Scottish Premiership, 1 Scottish Cup, 1 Dutch League, 1 Dutch Cup

D) 1 Dutch League, 1 Dutch Cup, 1 UEFA Cup

537. What is Virgil's date of birth?

A) 8th July 1991

B) 9th July 1992

C) 10th July 1993

D) 11th July 1994

538. What was the first individual award that Virgil won as a professional player?

A) Celtic FC Players' Player of the Year

B) Dutch Young Player of the Year

C) Scottish Player of the Year

D) Scottish Young Player of the Year

539. What are the main playing attributes of Virgil?

A) Complete midfielder with a wide range of skills, passing, shooting, tackling

B) Physically strong right-footed centre back who usually plays on the left side of central defence. Blessed with aerial ability, pace, and authority to lead the defence. Gifted technically to be able to pass and strike free kicks well

C) Tough-tackling defensive midfielder with ability to go on long dribbles, and shoot powerfully from long distance

D) Tricky winger with pace to burn

Alisson

540. What is Alisson's full name?

A) Alisson Ramses Becker

B) Alisson Becker

C) Alisson Ronald Becker

D) Alison Rivaldo Becker

541. What height is Alisson?

A) 6'1

B) 6'2

C) 6'3

D) 6'4

542. What is his date of birth?

A) 2nd October 1992

B) 10th October 1993

C) 18th October 1994

D) 26th October 1995

543. At which club did Alisson start his professional playing career?

A) Internacional

B) Inter Milan

C) AC Milan

D) Roma

544. From which club did Liverpool sign Alisson?

A) Internacional

B) Inter Milan

C) AC Milan

D) Roma

545. What was the transfer fee that Liverpool paid to sign Alisson?

A) £47.8 million

B) £55.8 million

C) £66.8 million

D) £74.8 million

546. Which country does Alisson play for?

A) Brazil

B) France

C) Germany

D) Portugal

547. From which country does Alisson's family descend from?

A) Brazil

B) France

C) Germany

D) Portugal

548. Which international tournament did Alisson win with his country (where he was given the award for best goalkeeper)?

A) World Cup

B) European Championship

C) Copa America

D) League of Nations

549. What are the main attributes of Alisson's game?

A) Bravery, good decision-making ability, leadership qualities, saving penalties, deep kicks, long throws

B) Fierce competitor, commanding presence, excellent reflexes, long reach, athletic, agile, ability to attack in the dying moments if his team are trailing

C) Positioning, distribution, consistency, shot stopping, ability to make crucial saves, ability to play out from the back. Strength, size, large powerful physique, agile, athletic, good reflexes

D) Slim, and flexible, stretching ability, catching crosses with one hand

Trent Alexander-Arnold

550. What is Trent Alexander-Arnold's middle name?

A) Alexander

B) James

C) John

D) Samuel

551. What is Alexander-Arnold's date of birth?

A) 7th October 1994

B) 7th October 1996

C) 7th October 1998

D) 7th October 2000

552. What is his height?

A) 5'9

B) 5'11

C) 6'1

D) 6'3

553. Which was the boyhood club of Alexander-Arnold?

A) Aston Villa

B) Everton

C) Liverpool

D) Nottingham Forest

554. How many clubs has Alexander-Arnold played for during his career?

A) 1

B) 2

C) 3

D) 4

555. What is Alexander-Arnold's shirt number?

A) 3

B) 6

C) 33

D) 66

556. What are Alexander-Arnold's playing attributes?

A) Amazing leadership quality, inspirational captain, strong competitor, physically imposing central defender

B) Hard-working defensive central midfielder, energetic, stamina, good all-round ability

C) Physical strength, speed, ability in the air, powerful, accurate shooting, holding up play, rising to the big occasion

D) One of the best attacking full-backs in world football due to his passing range, creative skill, crossing ability and set-piece deliveries

2018-19 Champions League

557. Who were the defending champions in the 2018-19 Champions League?

A) AC Milan

B) Atletico Madrid

C) Barcelona

D) Real Madrid

558. Who did Liverpool beat en-route to the 2019 Champions League final?

A) Bayer Leverkusen, Internazionale, Chelsea

B) Bayern Munich, Porto, Barcelona

C) Borussia Dortmund, Man City, Ajax

D) Man U, Bayern Munich, Ajax

559. In which city was the 2019 Champions League final played?

A) Amsterdam

B) Barcelona

C) Madrid

D) Lisbon

560. Who were Liverpool's opponents in the 2019 Champions League final?

A) Ajax

B) Bayern Munich

C) Real Madrid

D) Spurs

561. What was the half-time score of the 2019 Champions League final?

A) 1-0 to Liverpool

B) 2-0 to Liverpool

C) 0-1 to their opponents

D) 0-2 to their opponents

562. What was the score at full-time of the 2019 Champions League final?

A) 1-0 to Liverpool

B) 2-0 to Liverpool

C) 3-1 to Liverpool

D) 3-2 to Liverpool

563. Who scored Liverpool's first goal in the 2019 Champions League final?

A) Roberto Firmino

B) Sadio Mane

C) Divock Origi

D) Mo Salah

564. Who scored Liverpool's last goal in the 2019 Champions League final?

A) Roberto Firmino

B) Divock Origi

C) Sadio Mane

D) Mo Salah

565. Who was the man of the match of the 2019 Champions League final?

A) Virgil van Dijk

B) Jordan Henderson

C) Sadio Mane

D) Mo Salah

566. Who was the top scorer of the 2019 Champions League tournament?

A) Mane

B) Messi

C) Ronaldo

D) Salah

2019-20 Premier League title

567. Who were the reigning champions going into the 2019-20 Premier League season?

A) Arsenal

B) Leicester

C) Man City

D) Spurs

568. Before the league was suspended in March due to the global coronavirus pandemic, what was the points difference between Liverpool and second place?

A) 5

B) 10

C) 15

D) 25

569. During the season Liverpool achieved an English record-equalling ? consecutive winning matches.

A) 12

B) 14

C) 16

D) 18

570. Which team ended Liverpool's winning run?

A) Norwich City

B) Sheffield United

C) Watford

D) West Ham

571. What other record did Liverpool achieve during the season?

A) Biggest victory

B) Most consecutive home wins

C) Most consecutive away wins

D) Most goals scored in a game

572. The 2020 Premier League triumph means that Liverpool have won the Premier League how many times?

A) 1

B) 10

C) 16

D) 18

573. For how many years had Liverpool fans been waiting to be crowned Champions of England when they won the Premier League in 2020?

A) 10

B) 20

C) 30

D) 40

Thiago Alcantara

574. What is Thiago's full name?

A) Thiago Alcantara do Nascimento

B) Thiago Armando Alcantara

C) Thiago Andres Alcantara

D) Thiago Alemao Alcantara

575. What is Thiago's date of birth?

A) 7th March 1987

B) 17th March 1989

C) 11th April 1991

D) 22nd April 1993

576. What is Thiago's height?

A) 5'9

B) 5'10

C) 5'11

D) 6'

577. What is Thiago's nationality?

A) Argentinian

B) Brazilian

C) Peruvian

D) Spanish

578. In which country was Thiago born?

A) Colombia

B) Italy

C) France

D) Venezuela

579. What shirt number does Thiago wear for Liverpool?

A) 6

B) 16

C) 26

D) 36

580. What is the name of Thiago's father?

A) Macarino

B) Mauro Silva

C) Mazinho

D) Mourinho

581. Which of the following clubs has Thiago not played for?

A) Barcelona B

B) Barcelona

C) Bayern Munich

D) Red Bull Leipzig

582. With which club did Thiago start his youth career?

A) Arsenal

B) Barcelona

C) Flamengo

D) Red Bull Leipzig

583. How many Champions Leagues has Thiago won?

A) 0

B) 1

C) 2

D) 3

584. How many Club World Cups has Thiago won?

A) 0

B) 1

C) 2

D) 3

585. What is Thiago's style of play?

A) Creative, highly gifted playmaker, accurate distribution, excellent dribbling, ball-control, technique

B) False nine. A skilful, and tactically aware leader, and supremely dangerous attacker, able to score goals at a prolific rate, while also contributing assists

C) Hard tackling physically imposing muscular and aggressive centre back who has a no-nonsense approach to distribution

D) Skilful winger with a burst of pace, and a range of passes, skills, tricks, and accurate crosses

586. How much did Liverpool pay to sign Thiago? (without the £5 million in potential add-ons)

A) £20 million

B) £30 million

C) £40 million

D) £50 million

Diogo Jota

587. What nationality is Diogo Jota?

A) Argentinian

B) Brazilian

C) Portuguese

D) Spanish

588. What height is Jota?

A) 5’6

B) 5’8

C) 5’10

D) 6’

589. Where was Jota born?

A) Buenos Aires

B) Porto

C) Sao Paulo

D) Madrid

590. What is Jota’s date of birth?

A) 4th December 1992

B) 4th December 1994

C) 4th December 1996

D) 4th December 1998

591. What is Jota's squad number at Liverpool?

A) 20

B) 30

C) 40

D) 50

592. From which club did Liverpool sign Jota?

A) Atletico Madrid

B) Boca Juniors

C) Porto

D) Wolves

593. How much did Liverpool pay to sign Diogo Jota?

A) £21 million

B) £31 million

C) £41 million

D) £51 million

594. What are Jota's main playing attributes?

A) Attacking full back who is fierce, competitive, and has a great passing range, including accurate crosses

B) Complete box-to-box midfielder. Able to dictate tempo of games, and inspire by leading by example. Physical strength. Athleticism

C) Versatile, can play as an attacking midfielder, second striker, centre forward, left wing. Quick. Able to initiate counter-attacks. Excellent touch and ball control

D) Versatile defensive player, comfortable on the ball, professionalism, gifted technique

Roberto Firmino

595. What is the full name of Firmino?

A) Roberto Firmino Barbosa de Oliveira

B) Roberto Mauro Silva Firmino

C) Roberto Saldanho Firmino

D) Roberto Marcos Amaros Firmino

596. What is Firmino's date of birth?

A) 2nd October 1989

B) 2nd October 1991

C) 2nd October 1993

D) 2nd October 1995

597. What nationality is Firmino?

A) Argentinian

B) Brazilian

C) Chilean

D Venezuelan

598. With which club did Firmino start his senior playing career?

A) Chapecoense

B) Figueirense

B) Fortaleza

C) Vasco da Gama

599. Which club did Liverpool sign Firmino from?

A) Borussia Dortmund

B) Borussia Monchengladbach

C) Hoffenheim

D) Werder Bremen

. . .

600. What was the transfer fee paid by Liverpool to sign Firmino?

A) £9 million

B) £19 million

C) £29 million

D) £39 million

601. What height is Firmino?

A) 5'9

B) 5'11

C) 6'1

D) 6'3

602. What is Firmino's Liverpool squad number?

A) 7

B) 9

C) 17

D) 19

603. What is Firmino's style of play?

A) Comfortable on the ball, complete defender

B) Good in the air, creative, goalscorer, intelligence, creates space, energy, high work rate, contributes defensively

C) Hard-tackling full-back with electric pace and excellent dribbling, skills and vision to pick a pass

D) Old-fashioned winger who plays as close to the touchline and byline as possible. One of the best in the world for dribbling, and beating a marker through audacious skill

Ibrahima Konate

604. What nationality is Konate?

A) Belgium

B) Cameroon

C) France → france

D) Senegal

605. What is Konate's date of birth?

A) 7th December 1993

B) 13th January 1995

C) 19th March 1997

D) 25th May 1999

606. What is Konate's place of birth?

A) Berlin

B) Brussels

C) Cape Town

D) Paris Paris

607. How tall is White?

A) 5ft 10

B) 6ft

C) 6ft 2

D) 6ft 4

608. With which club did Konate start his senior playing career?

A) Hertha Berlin

B) Red Bull Leipzig

C) Sochaux

D) Paris Saint Germain

609. For which of the following clubs has Konate made 66 appearances?

A) Hertha Berlin

B) Red Bull Leipzig

C) Sochaux

D) Paris Saint Germain

610. What is Konate's squad number at Liverpool?

A) 5

B) 6

C) 15

D) 16

611. What was the approximate transfer fee that Liverpool paid to sign Konate?

A) £16 million

B) £26 million

C) £36 million

D) £46 million

612. What are Konate's main playing attributes?

A) Amazing leadership quality, inspirational captain, strong competitor, technical ability and a tough tackling style

B) Physical strength, speed, ability in the air, powerful, accurate shooting, holding up play, rising to the big occasion as a dynamic midfielder

C) Positional play, tackling, pace, strength, heading, passing

D) One of the best attacking full-backs in world football due to his passing range, creative skill, crossing ability, and set-piece deliveries

DEEP HISTORY ANSWERS

1A) Foundations and Achievements

1. C

2. A (former president of Everton)

3. D (they finished the season at the top of the table)

4. A

5. B

6. A

7. D

8. A

9. C

10. B

11. D

12. B

13. A

14. B

15. A

16. A

17. D

18. D

19. C

20. D

21. B

22. B

23. C

24. A

25. D

26. B

27. B

28. D

29. C

30. D

31. D (417)

32. B (17 from 1925 - 1936. Rush had 16, Fowler 10)

33. B

34. D

35. D (660, vs 515 and 620 for Dalglish and Hansen respectively)

36. A (628 vs 464 for Hypia and 338 for Riley)

37. C

38. C (1921-22 and 1922-23)

39. B (1947. They won none in the 1930s and 1950s)

40. C

41. D (6. They won 2 in the 1960s, and 4 in the 1970s)

42. D (1981)

43. C

44. C (47 in 1983-84. Salah has scored 44 in 2017-18. Hodgson scored 36 in 1930-31)

45. C (Coutinho, £142 million, and Suarez, £80 million)

46. B

47. C

48. D (It was in the 1951-52 FA Cup 4th Round)

49. C

50. C

51. B

52. D

53. D

54. B

55. C

56. C

57. D

58. C

59. C

60. D

61. D

62. C

63. C

64. D

65. C

66. D

67. B

68. B

69. C

70. C

71. D

72. D

1B) Walking with Giants - Bill Shankly

73. D

74. A

75. D

76. C

77. C

78. B

79. C

80. B

81. A

82. C

83. A (v Everton)

84. A

85. A

86. A

87. D

88. C (£180,000 from Arsenal in 1974)

89. A

90. B

91. C

92. C

93. B

94. C

95. C

96. B

97. C

98. B

99. B

100. B

101. A

102. B

103. B

104. C

105. C

106. C

107. B

108. D

109. C

110. B

111. A

112. A

113. C (1962)

114. B

115. D

116. D

117. A

118. A

119. C

120. D

121. B

122. D

123. D

124. B

125. C

126. A

127. A

128. A

129. D

130. A

131. C

132. C

133. B

134. B

135. B

136. B

137. A

138. B

139. C

140. A

141. C

142. C

143. B

144. A

145. B

146. A

147. A

148. B

149. A

150. C (1978, 1979)

151. D

152. D

153. A

154. B

155. D

156. A

157. A

158. A

159. B

1C) Walking with Giants - Bob Paisley

160. A

161. B

162. B

163. B

164. B

165. A

166. A

167. C

168. A

169. B

170. C

171. D

172. C

173. C

174. C

175. D

176. C

177. B

178. C

179. B

180. B

181. D

182. D

183. D

184. D

185. B

186. D

187. D

188. A

189. B

190. B

191. B

192. B

193. B

194. B

195. A

196. D

197. A

198. B

199. D

200. A

201. C

202. A

203. A

204. B

205. A (4)

206. B

207. C

208. B

209. B

210. C

211. B

212. C

213. B

214. D

215. A

216. A

217. B

218. D

219. A

220. A

221. A

222. B

223. A

224. C

225. A

226. C

227. D

227. C

228. C

229. A

230. A

231. B

232. D

TRIUMPHS AND DISASTERS ANSWERS

2A) The Red Machine

233. B

234. D

235. B

236. B

237. B

238. A (record fee for a teenager)

239. C

240. B

241. B

242. B

243. B

244. C

245. B

246. A

247. B

248. B

248. A

249. A

250. A

251. D

252. B

253. C

254. C

255. D

256. D

257. B

258. B

258. B

259. B

260. C

261. C

262. B

263. C

264. A

265. C

266. B

267. A (1984)

268. D

269. B

270. B

271. C

272. C

273. B

274. B

275. A

276. D

277. B

278. A

279. A

280. C

281. D

282. A

283. C

284. B

285. B (1987-88, and 1989-90)

286. A

287. C

288. A

289. C

290. B

291. A

292. B

293. D

294. D

295. D

296. A

297. B

298. A

299. A

300. D

301. A

302. C

303. C (Steve Staunton, Ronnie Whelan, Ray Houghton, John Aldridge)

304. B (Kevin Sheedy)

305. C (Ablett, Beardsley, Barnes, McMahon)

306. D (McDonald, Watson, Bracewell, Steven, Cottee)

307. A

308. C

309. A

310. C (£2.7m in 1988)

311. A

312. B

313. C

314. B

315. C

316. B

317. A

318. B (22 in league, 28 overall)

319. D

320. A

321. B

322. B

323. B

324. A (350 vs 307, 226, 166 for Evans, Houllier, and Rodgers respectively)

325. A

326. D

327. D

328. D

329. A

330. A

331. D

332. B

333. D

334. C

335. B

336. B

337. D

338. B

339. B

340. B

341. A

342. A

343. B

344. C

345. B

346. A

347. A

348. B

349. B

350. A

351. A

352. C

353. D

354. D

355. A

356. B

357. B

358. B

359. A

360. B

361. A

362. B

363. A

364. C

365. D

366. B

367. C

368. B

369. D

369. B

370. B

371. B

372. B

373. D

374. D

375. C

376. D

377. A

378. C

379. A

380. D

381. B

382. C

383. A

384. B

385. D

386. D

387. B

388. C

389. C

390. B

391. A

392. B

393. A

394. A

395. B

396. D

397. C

398. D

2B) Absolute Entertainment

399. C

400. B (the first FA Cup final to be played outside England, due to reconstruction of Wembley)

401. A

402. A

403. C

404. D

405. C

406. D

407. A

408. D

409. D

410. C

411. B

412. B

413. D (away against Stoke)

414. B

415. B

416. D

417. C

418. A

419. A

420. B

421. B

422. D

423. B

424. D

425. A

426. A

427. D

428. C

429. D

430. D

431. C

432. C

433. A (level with Inter Milan and Juventus)

434. C

435. D

436. C

437. B

438. D

439. D

440. A

441. A

442. C

443. A

444. B

445. C

446. B

447. B

448. D

449. B

450. D

451. B

452. B

453. C

454. C

455. D

456. A

457. B

458. B

459. D

460. B

461. C (4)

462. D

463. B

464. D

465. D

466. D

467. C

468. A

469. C

470. B

ULTRA-MODERN LIVERPOOL ANSWERS

3A) New Heights of Glory

471. C

472. D

473. D

474. D (£75 million)

475. B (£142 million)

476. A

477. A

478. D

479. B

480. C

481. D

482. C

483. C

484. D

485. D

486. A

487. D

488. B

489. A

490. A

491. A

492. B

493. C

494. B

495. D

496. B

497. D

498. B

499. A

500. D

501. D

502. C

503. C

504. B

505. D

506. B

507. B

508. C

509. B

510. B

511. A

512. A

513. C

514. C

515. C

516. B

517. D

518. B

519. A

520. C

521. B

522. D

523. B

524. B

525. D

526. A

527. B

528. B

529. A

530. C

531. B

532. D

533. A

534. A

535. D

536. A

537. A

538. A (2013-14)

539. B

540. A

541. C

542. A

543. A

544. D

545. C

546. A

547. C

548. C (2019)

549. C

550. C

551. C

552. A

553. C

554. A

555. D

556. D

557. D

558. B

559. C

560. D

561. B

562. B

563. D

564. B

563. A

564. B (12 goals)

565. A

566. B

567. C

568. D

569. D

570. C

571. B

572. A

573. C

574. A

575. C

576. A

577. D

578. B

579. A

580. C

581. D

582. C

583. C (2011 & 2020)

584. C (2011 & 2013)

585. A

586. A

587. C

588. C

589. B

590. C

591. A

592. C

593. C

594. C

595. A

596. B

597. B

598. B

599. C

600. C

601. B

602. B

603. B

604. C

605. D

606.D

607. D

608. C

609. B

610. A

611. C

612. C

GRADING

As an additional bonus, just for fun, here are some grades you can use to quantify your performance.

Each grade corresponds to a different version of a History of Liverpool FC.

The better you do, the better the history!

A*

80%+

Absolutely Excellent. You have smashed it!

A

70-79%

A very respectable score. Well done!

B

60-69%

Decent. But you can do better.

C

50-59%

Average. Keep going.

D

40-49%

Weak performance. Must do better.

D GRADE FAN

Liverpool are in the doldrums and have been for a number of years.

After the sterling work of Bill Shankly and Bob Paisley that generated trophies and global respect, the once-fabled club has recently toiled with maximum effort and minimal effect.

Since Paisley left the club in 1983, his successor Joe Fagan guided the club to a penalty shootout loss to Roma in 1984.

Since then, Liverpool have struggled - winning two more league titles (in 1986 and 1988) before being overtaken by Arsenal, who were, undoubtedly, the best English team of the early nineties, and their success was followed by an unprecedented spell of domestic domination by Manchester United.

Man U, Arsenal and Chelsea became the big three in English football until Manchester City's big money takeover in 2009 enabled them to muscle in on the Premier League trophy, winning it in 2012, 2014, 2018, 2019 and 2021.

Liverpool have still won more European Cups than any other British team (3), with Nottingham Forest and Manchester United second with two apiece and both Arsenal and Chelsea managing to get one each.

The big concern for Liverpool is their inability to win anything at all – their last European Cup having arrived four decades ago (in 1981), and their last league title being that which was won in 1988.

Also, of concern is the club's strategic vision, and the constant loss of their best players to rival clubs.

The list of the players they have sold includes Carragher (Everton), Sterling (Man City), Gerrard (Chelsea), Owen and McManaman (Real Madrid), Suarez, Salah and Mane (Barcelona), Alexander-Arnold (Borussia Dortmund).

At the present time, Jose Mourinho has taken the helm after recent unconvincing spells by Sam Allardyce, Carlo Ancelotti and Unai Emery.

Liverpool's current best players include Pickford, Richarlison, Pulisic, Shaquiri, and Origi.

C GRADE LIVERPOOL FAN

Liverpool are a faded power in the world of football.

Their Scottish manager, Bill Shankly, laid the foundations to all of their success by revolutionising the club in the 1960s.

Liverpool emerged from his inspirational leadership as a force to be reckoned with and, in the seventies, became the best team in Europe.

Their past achievements place them in good standing in terms of British football, having won four European Cups in the seventies and eighties, but they have failed to win any trophies since the year 1990.

The club has become a bit of a laughing stock managerially, with an apparently ever-revolving door of new recruits trying their hand at turning around the club's fortunes - Pochettino, Mourinho, Hodgson to name just three.

Also, several promising players cut short their Anfield careers citing concern at the way the club was being run, including Carragher (Everton), Gerrard (Chelsea), Fowler (Leeds), and Owen (Real Madrid).

Several clubs, such as Man U, Man City, Chelsea, Arsenal, and Spurs habitually finish above Liverpool in the league table.

Now, the Reds have invested heavily in youth with some ambitious signings.

Key players going forward are Trent Alexander-Arnold, Joe Gomez, Raheem Sterling, Sadio Mane, Roberto Firmino, Xherdan Shaqiri, Virgil Van Dijk and Alisson.

The Reds are managed by Nuno Gomes.

B GRADE LIVERPOOL FAN

Liverpool are a significant power in the world of football, but this is mainly based on their history and culture.

Their Scottish manager, Bill Shankly, laid the foundations to their following success by revolutionising the Anfield club in the 1960s.

Liverpool emerged from his inspirational leadership as a force to be reckoned with and, in the seventies, became the best team in Europe.

In the 1970s and 1980s, Liverpool's spell of four European Cups in eight years established them at the top table of club football, and their reign of power was only cut short by the ban on English clubs.

Since their golden spell during the 1970s and 1980s, Liverpool have struggled to maintain consistent success throughout the years that followed, yet have still managed to secure a

European Cup, two UEFA Cups, two FA Cups, two League Cups in the past 30 years.

Over the years, Liverpool's best players have included names such as Keegan, Dalglish, Kennedy, Souness.

In more recent times, their best players have come up through the youth system. Carragher, Gerrard, Fowler, Owen, McManaman immediately spring to mind, along with Raheem Sterling, a loyal servant to the club, and influential national figure on and off the pitch.

On the transfer front, Liverpool have not fared so well, with the impression being that Anfield is a club that players no longer take seriously as the club has fallen well behind the Manchester giants and London clubs, Spurs, Arsenal, and Chelsea.

One saving grace is that Liverpool have a relatively new manager with a unique and effective approach – Jurgen Klopp - who has succeeded in changing the mentality at Anfield and is now starting to see his young and exciting side, filled with a smattering of genuine world class players (Van Dijk, Salah, Mane, Firmino, Thiago, Alexander Arnold, Alisson), challenge at the very top of the Premier League table.

A GRADE LIVERPOOL SUPPORTER

Liverpool are a major power in the world of football.

Their Scottish manager, Bill Shankly, laid the foundations to all of their success by revolutionising the club in the 1960s.

Liverpool emerged from his inspirational leadership as a force to be reckoned with and, in the seventies, became the best team in Europe.

In the 1970s and 1980s, Liverpool's spell of four European Cups in eight years established the club as a football superpower, and their reign of power in Europe was only cut short by the UEFA ban on English clubs.

The Reds continued to be successful domestically until 1990. And since then have performed relatively well in cup competitions, winning the European Cup on two further occasions.

To date, Liverpool can boast a rich history in terms of motivation, magical European nights, and consistently playing good football and getting great results.

They have benefitted from managers with various philosophies and approaches - including the golden era of Shankly and Paisley, to present day icon: Jurgen Klopp.

Their first Premier League win came after an unprecedented global viral infection that shut down the game for a number of months mid-season of 2021-22.

Liverpool would love a 7th European Cup.

Over the years, their best players have included star names such as Keegan, Dalglish, Kennedy, Souness, Barnes, Rush, Suarez.

In the modern day, names like Alexander-Arnold, Mane, Salah, Jota, and Van Dijk are heralded by an international base of loyal, patient and passionate supporters.

A STAR LIVERPOOL MASTERMIND

Liverpool are, by far and away, the foremost power in the world of modern football.

Their Scottish manager, Bill Shankly laid the foundations to all of their following success by revolutionizing the club in the 1960s, giving Liverpool a brand new sense of fierce pride and powerful purpose.

In the 1970s and 1980s, an inspired Liverpool swept all before them, winning an unheard of eight consecutive European Cups from 1977 to 1984.

This astounding success meant that the Reds were able to exert great pulling power in the international transfer market.

Liverpool managed to secure the signings of both Ruud Gullit and Marco Van Basten who decided to end their careers at the Anfield club.

As well as a strong Dutch connection that saw Bergkamp, and Seedorf join the club and Cruyff take the helm as manager in the early 1990s, Liverpool also built firm links with German football as Beckenbauer also had a spell as manager and Kohler, Sammer, and Klinsmann all played for the club.

To this date, Liverpool's deep Dutch and German links continue to be strong with manager Jurgen Klopp, and club captain Virgil Van Dijk.

The Reds' progressive brand of football - a unique evolution of English, Scottish, Dutch, and German styles is what makes the club stand apart.

The "Liverpool Way" combines Scottish passing, English spiritedness, German resoluteness, and Dutch tactical awareness.

Astonishing success on the field has reflected a progressive attitude, with the club's haul including a formidable fifteen European Cups.

Liverpool's success has inspired English clubs to be the most successful in Europe with seven English clubs having won at least one European Cup: Man U, Spurs, Chelsea, Manchester City, Arsenal, Everton and Leeds United being the others.

Liverpool are truly the international gold standard for club football excellence.

REVIEW

Thank you for reading the *Amazing Liverpool Quiz*.

I hope you enjoyed it as much as I loved delving deep into the history of the club to bring it to you.

If you liked the book, it would be fantastic if you were able to write a quick review as this will help other Liverpool fans find it.

Your support is much appreciated!

JOIN THE CLUB!

Join the **Amazing LFC Members Club** to get free books and free additions/updates to books.

Members are always the first to hear about my new books and publications.

It is completely free to sign up and you will never be spammed by me, you can opt out easily at any time.

As a way of welcome, I will send you my 27 absolute best Liverpool video clips that complement this book perfectly and tell the *Story of Liverpool F.C.*

Go to offer.amazingsoccerbooks.com/liverpool to sign up.

ACKNOWLEDGEMENTS

For my family, and the worldwide Liverpool family.

You'll Never Walk Alone

ALSO BY JAMES CORMACK

The Amazing Liverpool Word Search Puzzle Book

The Amazing Liverpool Colouring Book

Coming Soon:

The Amazing Liverpool Crossword Book

COPYRIGHT

Published by Amazing Soccer Books, United Kingdom, in 2021.
www.amazingsoccerbooks.com
www.facebook.com/amazingsoccerbooks
eBook ISBN: 978-1-914200-05-2
ISBN: 978-1-914200-11-3

Cover Design by Ricardo Gomez
Cover Illustration by Pedro Hernandez

We are grateful for the people depicted in this book for providing us with the inspiration to create it, and would welcome any relevant persons, including the people depicted in our artistic impressions, reaching out to us.

10% of the 2021 profits from Amazing Soccer Books will be donated to the World Health Organization Coronavirus Fund. For more information please visit https://www.who.int/emergencies/diseases/nover-coronavirus-2019/donate

Printed in Great Britain
by Amazon

72460815R00169